Welcome

Actually, all education is self-education. A teacher is only a guide, to point out the way, and no school, no matter how excellent, can give you education. What you receive is like the outlines in a child's coloring book. You must fill in the colors yourself.

—Louis L'Amour

When the idea of writing a book about coloring techniques came to me it seemed too simple of an idea. And yet, the idea of teaching coloring techniques would not go away. More and more, friends were approaching me with questions about how to color, how to achieve a certain look, or the steps to create that technique. Soon they were asking for classes in a large range of mediums. I would often laugh them off and say, "Just come on over, and we will sit and color together. You don't need a class; you just need a few tips and a bit of practice!" As I sat at my desk planning, prepping and researching, my approach to this was as simple as the concepts I wanted to write about. I wanted you to feel you were just spending an afternoon with a friend, while gathering some new tips and techniques on coloring.

Our planning team spent many hours working on each aspect of this book. We honed in on what we considered to be the most popular coloring mediums as they relate to paper crafting, the idea of coloring techniques, and what exactly you would want in a coloring-technique book. As we compared notes we all found that at the top of our list were three main coloring mediums: watercolor, colored pencil, and the newest rage to hit the paper-crafting market, alcohol-based-ink markers. With a well-defined focus

established for our book, it was time to assemble the designer team. We were looking for designers with very specific talents, and we assembled a wonderful team who we feel represent some of the best colorist designers in the industry. The product of all this "behind the scenes work" now sits in your hands. We hope you find the instructions clear and concise, the tips and techniques helpful, and the projects nothing short of inspiring. We invite you to gather your supplies and come spend the afternoon with us, learning to color your world in a whole new way.

Writer Bio

Keri Lee Sereika, currently living in South Carolina, is a stay at home mother of four and wife to a USAFR pilot. She has authored crafting articles for a variety of magazines and online media, and has had her designs featured in numerous publications. When she's not busy playing with her kids, you'll find Keri in her studio creating projects or researching and writing articles on crafting.

Contents

Colored-Pencil Techniques

The craving for color is a natural necessity just as for water and fire. Color is a raw material indispensable to life. At every era of his existence and his history, the human being has associated color with his joys, his actions and his pleasures."

—Frenand Leger

If the idea of trying to blend color using a brush and water makes you skittish, perhaps a better medium to start with would be colored pencil. A quick look at the difference in pencil qualities as well as how the quality of the colored pencils used will affect the outcome of the finished piece, will help you decide which type of colored pencil is best suited for this technique.

The "lead" or core of a colored pencil is comprised of a mixture of pigment, wax and fillers. The ratio of color pigment to wax and filler depends heavily on the quality of colored pencil used. Typically, artist-quality colored pencils have a higher pigment to wax and filler ratio. The "leads" tend to be softer, and you can control the amount of color you apply to your image simply by how much pressure you apply when coloring with them. While the technique demonstrated, and many of the samples shown, will be utilizing artist-quality colored pencils, use what you have on hand for learning these techniques. If you only have "craft quality" colored pencils, the biggest difference you will notice is that the pigment to wax and filler ratio is much lower,

causing the leads to be harder. When coloring with craft-quality colored pencils you will find that they do not leave as much pigment and often need additional layers and applications of color to achieve the depth of color you are looking for.

The wax-based "leads" of colored pencils can be broken down using a blending agent called artist-grade odorless mineral spirits (OMS). The color can then be blended or moved along the surface of the paper using a tool called an artist blending stump. A blending stump is a tool formed of compressed paper pulp. The pulp is pressed into a dense tube and sharpened at both ends. It can be sharpened and cleaned using a sanding block or sandpaper pad. When looking for artist blending stumps, do not be fooled into purchasing tortillions. Tortillions are also used for blending, but they are tightly wrapped, hollow, paper blending instruments. And while they are created for blending, they will not soak up the blending agent the way a blending stump will; therefore, they will not produce the same outcome.

When working with colored pencils it doesn't really matter what type of ink you use to stamp your image, but you will need a good smooth-surfaced card stock for ease of blending. A good smooth-surfaced card stock with tightly woven fibers allows the pigment to be broken down and blended across the surface, whereas a lesser quality, rougher-surfaced card stock can be difficult to work with because the pigment tends to stay where you put it and will not blend out as nicely.

1. Begin by stamping your image and choosing which colors you plan on working with. It will be helpful to have multiple blending stumps to work with so that you do not have to sand as much between color changes and color applications.

2. Apply a heavy line of color to the left side of the areas you choose to color with your first color.

3. Roll or dip the tip of your blending stump into the odorless mineral spirits (OMS) until it is fully saturated,

but not dripping. ***Note:*** *If you are wary of working with odorless mineral spirits, are pregnant or have an allergy to it, pure baby oil can be used instead for this technique. It must be used sparingly so as to not stain the image you are working on, so a bit of experimentation should be done to find out just how much oil is needed to break down the wax and fillers in the colored pencil leads.*

4. Using small circular motions, blend the color into the open white area of the image.

5. Using a sanding block or sandpaper pad, clean the first color off the tip of your blending stump before applying and blending the next color.

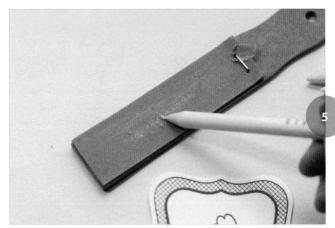

6. Apply and blend additional colors as shown, repeating steps 2–5 for each color.

7. Once you have colored your image, reapply a second layer of color to deepen the saturation until the desired color level is reached. Again, blend just as before using blending stumps and OMS.

8. Apply a thick line of color all the way around the inner edge of the frame image.

9. As a finishing touch, use a larger, fatter stump and OMS to blend the color inward toward the fish image. Be sure to stop just before reaching the fish to allow for a small halo of white to remain. This will cause the fish image to really "pop" and stand out.

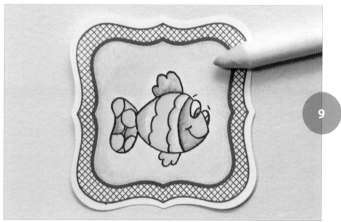

Use your colored image to create your finished project.

Happy Birthday Fishes

Design by **Keri Lee Sereika**

Form a 6 x 6-inch top-folded card from green card stock. Cut a 5⅝ x 5⅝-inch square of printed paper. Adhere argyle side faceup to dark blue card stock; trim a small border. Adhere centered to card front.

Cut a 5⅛ x 5⅛-inch square of printed paper. Adhere floral side faceup to dark blue card stock; trim a border. Wrap ribbon around square as shown; tie a bow; trim ends. Pierce two holes in upper right corner of square; attach blue rhinestone brads. Using foam squares, attach panel to card front as shown.

Using Classic Scalloped Squares SM die template, die-cut a 3⅛ x 3⅛-inch scalloped square from light green card stock. Pierce a hole in each corner of scalloped square and attach silver round brads.

Using Labels One die template, die-cut a 2⅞ x 2⅞-inch label from white card stock. Using blue ink, stamp label frame onto label. Stamp fish onto label with black ink. Color fish and label background with colored pencils, using mineral spirits and blending stump to blend colors. Using foam squares, attach to scalloped square. Attach to card front with foam squares.

Using Labels Four die template, die-cut a ⅞ x 1⅜-inch label from cream card stock. Stamp "happy birthday!" onto label with blue ink. Use foam squares to attach label to lower left area of card front. ✗

Sources: *Card stock from Bazzill Basics Paper Inc.; printed paper from Fancy Pants Designs; stamp sets from Gina K. Designs; chalk ink pads from Clearsnap Inc.; colored pencils from Prismacolor; die templates from Spellbinders™ Paper Arts.*

Materials

- Card stock: green, light green, dark blue, white, cream
- Summer Soiree Beach House double-sided printed paper
- Stamp sets: Just Keep Swimming, Tag, You're It!, Lovely Labels
- Chalk ink pads: blue, black
- Colored pencils: chartreuse, aquamarine, indigo blue, true blue
- Odorless mineral spirits
- Blending stumps
- Sandpaper pad
- Brads: 4 silver round, 2 blue rhinestone decorative
- 22 inches ⅝-inch-wide green/white dot ribbon
- Die templates: Labels One (#S4-161), Labels Four (#S4-190), Classic Scalloped Squares SM (#S4-129)
- Die-cutting machine
- Piercing tool
- Adhesive foam squares
- Paper adhesive

You're Too Cool!

Design by **Keri Lee Sereika**

Form a 4½ x 6¼-inch side-folded card from brown card stock.

Cut a 4¼ x 2½-inch piece of Science Fair paper. Cut a 4¼ x 3¾-inch piece of Chicken Coop paper. Adhere printed papers together so they form a 4¼ x 6-inch paper panel. Using sewing machine, zigzag-stitch paper panel to card front as shown.

Cut a 4⅛ x ¾-inch strip of light green card stock, adhere to card front over paper seam. Pierce two holes on each end of card-stock strip; attach brads.

Die-cut a 3 x 2⅜-inch label and a 1⅛ x ⅞-inch label from white card stock. Stamp Bug Hammock onto larger label; color with colored pencils. Use mineral spirits and blending stumps to blend colors. Detail bug's wings with glitter glue. Adhere to dark brown card stock, trim a small border. Using foam squares, attach label to card front as shown.

Stamp "You're too cool!" onto smaller label; pierce a hole through top of label. Slide a brad through photo hanger and through label hole; secure brad closed. String ribbon through photo hanger; tie knot and trim ends. Using foam squares, attach label to lower right corner of card front. Secure bow with an adhesive dot. ✘

Sources: Card stock from Bazzill Basics Paper Inc.; printed papers from October Afternoon; stamps from Inky Antics; chalk ink pad from Clearsnap Inc.; colored pencils from Prismacolor; die templates from Spellbinders™ Paper Arts.

Materials

- Card stock: brown, dark brown, light green, white
- Double-sided printed papers: Report Card Science Fair, Farm Fresh Chicken Coop
- Stamps: Bug Hammock, Too Cool
- Black chalk ink pad
- Colored pencils: jasmine, lime peel, deco blue, light cerulean blue, violet blue, peach, light umber, deco aqua, French grey 30%
- Odorless mineral spirits
- Blending stumps
- Sandpaper pad
- 5 small copper brads
- Copper photo hanger
- 3 inches ⅝-inch-wide aqua/white dot satin ribbon
- Large Labels die templates (#S4-168)
- Die-cutting machine
- Sewing machine with cream thread
- Piercing tool
- Clear glitter glue
- Adhesive foam squares
- Adhesive dots
- Paper adhesive

Baby's Window

Design by **Kathy Menzies**

Form a 5¼ x 5¼-inch top-folded card from white card stock.

Cut a 5 x 5-inch square of floral striped paper. Cut a 5 x 2-inch strip of brown printed paper and a 5 x 1¾-inch strip of pink printed paper. Adhere pink strip to brown strip. Wrap a 7-inch length of ribbon around layered strip; secure ribbon ends to back. Adhere layered strip to floral striped square 1½ inches above bottom edge. Adhere square to light blue card stock; trim a small border. Adhere to card front.

Cut a 2⅞ x 3⅝-inch rectangle from off-white card stock. Using black ink, stamp Animals in Window image onto rectangle; color with colored pencils. Blend colors using mineral spirits and blending stumps. Add glitter glue to cloud. Apply Flower Soft Glue to bunnies' tails; add white sprinkles.

Adhere stamped rectangle to light green card stock; trim a small border. Using foam tape, attach rectangle to light blue card stock; trim a small border. In the same manner, attach layered rectangle to card front, as shown.

Form a bow with remaining ribbon by folding ends to middle of length and overlapping ends. String button with thread; wrap thread around center of bow and tie a knot. Using double-sided tape, attach bow to right side of card front as shown.

Stamp "Bitty Blessing" onto white card stock with light blue ink. Using tag punch, punch stamped area. Punch hole through top of tag; insert thread through hole. Wrap thread around thread on back of button; tie knot. Trim ends. ✗

Sources: *Card stock from Paper Temptress, Papertrey Ink, and Memory Box; printed papers from BasicGrey; stamp from Rubbernecker Stamp Co.; stamp set from Papertrey Ink; white sprinkles and Flower Soft Glue from Flower Soft Inc.; colored pencils from Prismacolor, Faber-Castell USA Inc. and Lyra; Scallop Tag punch from Martha Stewart Crafts; glitter glue from Ranger Industries Inc.*

Materials

- Card stock: white, light blue, light green, off-white
- Printed papers: floral striped floral, brown, pink
- Stamps: Animals in Window, Bitty Baby Blessings set
- Dye ink pads: light blue, black
- Colored pencils: blush pink, lime peel, bronze, cloud blue, cool grey 10%, cool grey 50%, cream, sandbar brown, light umber, ginger root, espresso, light ultramarine, rose carmine, blue violet, dark violet, lemon cadmium
- Odorless mineral spirits
- Blending stumps
- Sandpaper pad
- White sprinkles
- 14 inches 1½-inch-wide green/white dot grosgrain ribbon
- Large white button
- White thread
- Punches: Scalloped Tag, ¹⁄₁₆-inch hole
- Flower Soft Glue
- Glitter glue
- Double-sided tape
- Adhesive foam tape
- Paper adhesive

Fairy Thanks

Design by **Jeanne Streiff**

Form a 4¼ x 5½-inch top-folded card from white card stock; ink edges brown. Cut a 2 x 5⅛-inch strip of metallic gold card stock; adhere to left side of card front. Adhere gold beads to card front, two to upper left corner and two to lower left corner.

Using black ink, stamp fairy and flower image onto white card stock. Die-cut stamped area with a 3¼-inch circle die template; with die template still in place, sponge brown ink onto circle. Color image with colored pencils, blending colors with mineral spirits and blending stumps; accent with glitter pens.

Die-cut a 3⅝-inch scalloped circle from dark brown card stock. Adhere stamped circle to scalloped circle; attach to card front as shown. Using brown ink, stamp "Thanks!" onto lower right corner of card front. ✘

Sources: Card stock from Couture Cardstock; stamps from Stamp N Plus Scrap N; Spica glitter pens from Imagination International Inc.; colored pencils from Prismacolor; die templates from Spellbinders™ Paper Arts.

Materials

- Card stock: white, metallic gold, dark brown
- Stamps: Black-Eyed Susan Fairies, Note-Ables set
- Dye ink pads: black, brown
- Glitter pens: lemon, clear
- Colored pencils: light peach, sunburst yellow, yellow-orange, chestnut, chocolate, moss green, warm grey 30%, warm grey 50%, white
- Odorless mineral spirits
- Blending stumps
- Sandpaper pad
- 4 gold flat-back metal beads
- Die templates: Standard Circles LG (#S4-114), Classic Scallop Circles LG (#S4-124)
- Die-cutting machine
- Craft sponge
- Adhesive foam squares
- Paper adhesive

Special Friend

Design by **Asela Hopkins**

Form a 4 x 9⅛-inch side-folded card from green card stock; ink edges brown. Cut two 4 x 2¼-inch rectangles from printed paper. Using piercing tool and template, pierce a line of holes ⅜ inch from one long edge of both rectangles. Adhere to card front as shown.

Cut a 3¼ x 5⅛-inch rectangle from tan card stock; ink edges brown. Pierce holes in four corners. Stamp grapes with black ink onto tan rectangle; color with markers. Detail grapes and center of leaves with colored pencils, using mineral spirits and blending stumps to blend colors. Outline grapes with anise marker. Using black ink, stamp "Special friend" under grapes.

Cut a 3½ x 5½-inch piece of ivory card stock; ink edges brown. Adhere stamped rectangle to ivory rectangle. Using foam dots, attach rectangle to card front as shown. ✗

Sources: *Card stock and stamp set from Gina K. Designs; printed paper from Webster's Pages; Palette fast-drying ink pad from Stewart Superior Corp.; colored pencils from Prismacolor; Copic markers from Imagination International Inc.*

Materials

- Card stock: green, ivory, tan
- Postcards from Paris Romantique Chic double-sided printed paper
- Fruitful Harvest stamp set
- Ink pads: black fast-drying, brown dye
- Markers: yellow-green, anise, pale lilac
- Colored pencils: white matches, marine green
- Odorless mineral spirits
- Blending stumps
- Sandpaper pad
- Craft sponge
- Piercing tool and template
- Adhesive foam dots
- Paper adhesive

Materials

- Card stock: white, off-white, dark purple, sage green
- Wisteria printed papers: Finch, Garden Patio
- Stamp sets: In Bloom, With Sympathy, Very Vintage Labels No. 5
- Dye ink pads: brown, olive green, purple
- Watermark ink pad
- Clear embossing powder
- Colored pencils: raspberry, black cherry, cream, green gold, olive green yellowish
- Odorless mineral spirits
- Blending stumps
- Sandpaper pad
- 6 inches ⅝-inch-wide purple grosgrain ribbon
- Punches: Flourish Edge, Sunburst Border
- Die templates: Labels Five (#S4-229), Long Classic Rectangles SM (#S4-144)
- Die-cutting machine
- Embossing heat tool
- Glitter glue
- Adhesive foam tape
- Paper adhesive

Jeweled Peony

Design by **Kathy Menzies**

Form a 6 x 6-inch top-folded card from white card stock. Using Flourish Edge punch, punch center on each edge of card front except for top edge.

Cut a 5¼ x 5¼-inch piece of Garden Patio paper and adhere to dark purple card stock; trim a small border. Adhere to sage green card stock; trim a small border. Adhere centered to card front.

Cut a 5¼ x 2½-inch strip of sage green card stock; punch bottom edge with Sunburst Border punch. Adhere a 5¼ x 1½-inch strip of Finch paper over punched strip. Wrap ribbon over layered strip as shown; secure ends to back. Using foam tape, attach layered strip to card front 1¾ inches from bottom edge.

Using brown ink, stamp two large peonies, a small peony and two leaves onto off-white card stock. Color with colored pencils, blending colors with blending stumps and mineral spirits. Cut out stamped images, cutting out only the center of one large peony. Detail peony center with glitter glue; set aside to dry.

Stamp label onto off-white card stock using olive green ink. Use watermark ink to stamp label on top of olive green label; sprinkle embossing powder on top of label and heat-emboss using embossing heat tool.

Die-cut embossed image using 3⅓ x 3⅝-inch Labels Five die template. Adhere embossed label to dark purple card stock; trim a small border. Using 3⅝ x 4⅛-inch Labels Five die template, die-cut a label from sage green card stock. Adhere layered embossed label to sage green label with foam tape.

Attach peony center to large peony with foam tape. In the same manner, attach peony to labels. Adhere remaining leaves and small peony to labels as shown. Attach centered to card front with foam tape.

Using purple ink, stamp sentiment onto white card stock. Die-cut stamped area using 2½ x 1⅛-inch Long Classic Rectangles SM die template. Adhere to sage green card stock; trim a small border. Adhere to card front, tucked under labels, as shown. ✗

Sources: Card stock from Paper Temptress and Die Cuts With A View; printed papers from BasicGrey; In Bloom and With Sympathy stamp sets from Papertrey Ink; Very Vintage Labels No. 5 stamp set from Waltzingmouse Stamps; colored pencils from Prismacolor and Faber-Castell USA Inc.; Flourish Edge punch from Martha Stewart Crafts; Sunburst Border punch from Fiskars; glitter glue from Ranger Industries Inc.

Blue Hydrangea

Design by **Asela Hopkins**

Form a 4¼ x 5½-inch side-folded card from blue card stock. Cut a 4⅛ x 5¼-inch piece of green dot paper; adhere to card front. Cut a 3⅝ x 4¾-inch piece of Frond Epiphany paper; adhere to card front as shown.

Stamp hydrangea onto a 3¼ x 4-inch piece of white card stock; color with colored pencils. Use mineral spirits and blending stumps to blend colors.

Stamp hydrangea onto white card stock. Color only the flower with colored pencils; blend colors. Cut out flower. Using foam dots, attach flower over complete hydrangea image. Adhere to card front as shown.

Decorate card front with rickrack and pearls as desired. ✗

Sources: *White card stock from Neenah Paper Inc.; Frond Epiphany printed paper from Memory Box; Palette fast-drying ink pad from Stewart Superior Corp.; colored pencils from Prismacolor.*

Materials

- Card stock: white, blue
- Printed papers: Frond Epiphany, green dot
- Hydrangea stamp
- Black fast-drying ink pad
- Colored pencils: chartreuse, non-photo blue, violet blue, canary yellow, olive green
- Odorless mineral spirits
- Blending stumps
- Sandpaper pad
- 4¼ inches ⅜-inch-wide green rickrack
- 4 self-adhesive pearls
- Adhesive foam dots
- Paper adhesive

Pixie Thinking of You

Design by **Chrissy Le**

Form a 4¼ x 5½-inch side-folded card from yellow card stock.

Using embossing machine and Floral Fantasy embossing folder, emboss a 4 x 5⅜-inch rectangle of white card stock. Adhere centered to card front.

Cut a 3½ x 4¾-inch rectangle from white card stock. Emboss using Swiss Dots embossing folder; punch bottom edge with Doily Lace Edge punch. Wrap cream ribbon around rectangle as shown, securing ends to back. Adhere centered to card front with foam squares.

Using computer and printer, print fairy image and "Thinking of You" onto white card stock leaving space between image and sentiment. Punch sentiment using Word Window punch; color using yellow chalk. Die-cut fairy image using 3⅛-inch Labels Three die template. With die template still in place, color fairy background using blue chalk; remove die template. Color fairy image using markers, and add highlights and shading to the image with colored pencils. Use mineral spirits and blending stumps to blend colors. Detail fairy's wings using glitter glue.

Die-cut a 3¼-inch circle from yellow card stock. Adhere fairy label to yellow circle. Attach to card front using foam squares as shown.

Punch three small butterflies from white card stock. Adhere a rhinestone to each butterfly. Adhere to card front as shown. Tie a bow with white ribbon; trim ends; adhere to card front as shown. Attach white flower bead to center of bow.

Using foam squares, attach sentiment centered over cream ribbon. ✗

Sources: *Digital stamp from Pollycraft; colored pencils from Prismacolor; Copic markers from Imagination International Inc.; chalk from Pebbles Inc.; Word Window punch from Stampin' Up!; 3-in-1 Classic Butterfly punch and Doily Lace Edge punch from Martha Stewart Crafts; die templates from Spellbinders™ Paper Arts; Cuttlebug machine and embossing folders from Provo Craft; Stickles glitter glue from Ranger Industries Inc.*

Materials

- Card stock: yellow, white
- Lilybean Fairies Clover I Believe… digital stamp
- Markers
- Colored pencils
- Odorless mineral spirits
- Blending stumps
- Sandpaper pad
- Chalks: yellow, blue
- Satin ribbons: 5 inches ⅜-inch-wide cream, 3 inches ⅛-inch-wide white
- 3 red self-adhesive rhinestones
- White self-adhesive flower bead
- Punches: Word Window, 3-in-1 Classic Butterfly, Doily Lace Edge
- Die templates: Labels Three (#S4-189), Standard Circles LG (#S4-114)
- Embossing folders: Floral Fantasy (#37-1806), Swiss Dots (#37-1604)
- Die-cutting and embossing machine
- Iridescent clear glitter glue
- Adhesive foam squares
- Paper adhesive
- Computer with printer

Thinking of You

Fond Memories

Design by **Dawn Lusk**

Project note: *Use multiple blending stumps dedicated to color families to avoid mixing colors when blending. When coloring sky and clouds, hold colored pencil flat to image; draw squiggly lines and blend.*

Form a 5 x 5-inch top-folded card from olive green card stock. Die-cut bottom portion of card front with Lattice die template.

Cut a 4¾ x 4¾-inch square from light brown card stock. Using embossing folder and embossing machine, emboss bottom 1⅝ inch of one edge. Adhere to reverse side of card front so embossed portion can be seen on front of card.

Stamp a barn and a tree on scrap paper; cut out to create stamping masks.

Using Top Note die template, die-cut shape once each from white, dark brown and light brown card stocks. Set both brown die cuts aside.

Stamp barn onto white die-cut shape. Place barn mask on top of stamped barn. Stamp trees and grass around barn as desired. With barn mask still in place, mask one tree. Stamp sun, overlapping masked tree. Remove all masks.

With colored pencils, color and then blend one stamped image at a time. Detail barn trim, windowpanes and area where sunlight would hit trees with white gel pen. Color barn door hardware with bronze gel pen.

Cut both brown die cuts into four pieces from points. Adhere pieces to back of stamped die cut as shown.

Using largest die templates in Classic Ovals LG and SM sets, die-cut a ring from olive green card stock. Adhere to stamped area as shown.

Pierce holes at each point of layered die cuts and attach brads.

Stamp "Fond Memories" onto light brown card stock. Cut out and round corners with scissors. Adhere to layered die cuts as shown. Attach to card front using foam tape. ✘

Sources: *Card stock from Bazzill Basics Paper Inc. and Georgia-Pacific; stamp set from Innovative Stamp Creations Inc.; ink pad from Tsukineko LLC; colored pencils from Prismacolor; gel pens from Sakura of America and Zebra Pen Corp.; brads from Hobby Lobby Stores Inc.; die templates from Spellbinders™ Paper Arts and Sizzix/Ellison; Cuttlebug machine and embossing folder from Provo Craft.*

Materials

- Card stock: white, olive green, dark brown, light brown
- Farm Life stamp set
- Black ink pad
- Colored pencils: sienna brown, dark brown, sepia, black, burnt ochre, terra cotta, dark green, warm grey, French grey, apple green, grass green, spring green, deco yellow, yellow ochre, crimson red, sunburst yellow, deco blue
- Gel pens: white, bronze
- Odorless mineral spirits
- Blending stumps
- Sandpaper pad
- 4 copper decorative brads
- Die templates: Classic Ovals SM (#S4-112), Classic Ovals LG (#S4-110), Lattice Borderabilities® Petite (#S4-218), Top Note (#113463)
- Argyle embossing folder (#37-1603)
- Die-cutting and embossing machine
- Piercing tool
- Adhesive foam tape
- Paper adhesive

Fond Memories

Simple Argyle

Design by **Keri Lee Sereika**

Form a 4 x 9¼-inch side-folded card from blue-gray card stock. Cut a 3¾ x 9-inch piece of brown card stock; adhere centered to card front.

Cut a 3½ x 8¾-inch rectangle of tan card stock. Pierce three holes in upper right corner of rectangle and attach copper brads. Cut a 3½ x 1⅛-inch strip of dark brown card stock; adhere to rectangle as shown. Wrap blue ribbon around rectangle over dark brown strip; tie in knot; V-notch ends. Adhere rectangle to card front as shown.

Die-cut three 1⁷⁄₁₆ x 1⁷⁄₁₆-inch scalloped squares from dark brown card stock. Stamp stitched argyle square onto white textured card stock three times; color with colored pencils. Cut out squares; adhere to scalloped squares. Using foam squares, attach squares to card front as shown.

Stamp "For You" in lower right corner of card front. ✗

Sources: Card stock from Bazzill Basics Paper Inc.; stamp set from Impression Obsession Inc.; chalk ink pad from Clearsnap Inc.; colored pencils from Prismacolor; die template from Spellbinders™ Paper Arts.

Materials

- Card stock: white textured, tan, brown, dark brown, blue-gray
- Masculine stamp set
- Dark brown chalk ink pad
- Colored pencils: dark umber, slate grey
- 3 small copper brads
- 13 inches ⅞-inch-wide blue satin ribbon
- Classic Scalloped Squares SM die template (#S4-129)
- Die-cutting machine
- Piercing tool
- Adhesive foam squares
- Paper adhesive

Daisies & Roses

Design by **Debbie Olson**

Form a 4¼ x 5½-inch side-folded card from cream card stock.

Adhere a 4 x 2-inch piece of Farmers Market paper to a 4 x 5¼-inch piece of Needs Paint paper as shown. Using sewing machine, zigzag-stitch along top and bottom edges of Farmers Market rectangle. Adhere paper panel to a 4⅛ x 5⅜-inch piece of red card stock; machine-stitch along edge of Needs Paint paper. Wrap ribbon around panel as shown; tie a bow; trim ends. Adhere to card front as shown.

Die-cut a 2⅞-inch label from cream card stock; ink edges light tan. Using black ink, stamp flowers onto label. Stamp a Vintage Label frame onto label using light aqua ink. Color image with colored pencils, blending colors with mineral spirits and blending stumps. Attach to card front as shown with foam tape.

String button with thread; tie knot in back and trim ends. Adhere to card front as shown. ✗

Sources: Card stock and Vintage Labels stamp set from Papertrey Ink; Early Bird printed paper from Cosmo Cricket; The Thrift Shop printed paper from October Afternoon; Roses, Daisies & Polka Dots stamp from Lockhart Stamp Co.; colored pencils from Prismacolor; die template from Spellbinders™ Paper Arts.

Materials

- Card stock: cream, red
- Printed papers: Early Bird Farmers Market, The Thrift Shop Needs Paint
- Stamps: Roses, Daises & Polka Dots, Vintage Labels set
- Ink pads: black dye, light tan dye, light aqua pigment
- Colored pencils: white, cool grey 10%, cool grey 20%, cool grey 60%, cool grey 70%, light aqua, deco blue, deco aqua, scarlet lake, crimson lake, mahogany red, deco yellow, yellowed orange, chartreuse, apple green, olive green
- Odorless mineral spirits
- Blending stumps
- Sandpaper pad
- 20 inches 1¼-inch-wide red ribbon
- Aqua button
- Labels One die template (#S4-161)
- Die-cutting machine
- Sewing machine with cream thread
- Adhesive foam tape
- Paper adhesive

Meowy Christmas

Design by **Keri Lee Sereika**

Form a 4½ x 5½-inch side-folded card from green card stock. Cut a 4 x 5¼-inch piece of red/green/cream printed paper; adhere centered to card front. Cut a 4 x 1¼-inch strip of dark green card stock; crimp with paper crimper. Adhere to card front as shown.

Die-cut a 3⅞ x 2¾-inch label from white card stock and a 4⅝ x 3⅜-inch label from red card stock. Stamp Ornament Kitty onto white label; color with colored pencils. Use mineral spirits and blending stumps to blend colors. Stamp sentiment below kitty. Wrap ribbon around white label as shown; tie a knot and trim ends. Using foam squares, attach white label to red label. Attach labels to card front using foam squares. Place pearls onto card front as shown. ✗

***Sources:** Card stock from Bazzill Basics Paper Inc.; Hannah Scrap Pad from K&Company; stamps from Inky Antics; chalk ink pad from Clearsnap Inc.; colored pencils from Prismacolor; die templates from Spellbinders™ Paper Arts.*

Materials

- Card stock: green, dark green, red, white
- Hannah Scrap Pad
- Stamps: Ornament Kitty, Meowy Christmas
- Black chalk ink pad
- Colored pencils: green, dark green, light peach, crimson red, warm gray 20%, yellow ochre
- Odorless mineral spirits
- Blending stumps
- Sandpaper pad
- 4 self-adhesive white pearls
- 8 inches ¼-inch-wide green grosgrain ribbon
- Paper crimper
- Labels Eight die template (#S5-019)
- Die-cutting machine
- Adhesive foam squares
- Paper adhesive

Beary Happy Birthday

Design by **Chrissy Le**

Form a 5 x 6⅛-inch side-folded card from brown metallic card stock. Cut a 5⅞ x 6⅞-inch rectangle from Pulled Taffy paper; adhere to card front as shown.

Cut a 4½ x 4¾-inch piece of Orange Slices paper. Cut a 4¼ x 1-inch strip of orange card stock; punch bottom edge with Effervescence border punch. Adhere punched strip to bottom edge of Orange Slices piece on reverse side. Adhere layered rectangle to light yellow card stock; trim a small border. Wrap a 6-inch piece of ribbon around layered rectangle as shown; secure ends to back. Adhere centered to card front.

Print Birthday Bears, "Have a," "Beary" and "Happy Birthday!" onto white card stock, leaving space between each. Die-cut a 3⅝-inch blossom around Birthday Bear image, a ⅞-inch blossom around "Have a" and "Beary." Punch out "Happy Birthday!" using Word Window punch. Color backgrounds of all pieces using yellow chalk. Color bears as desired using markers, and add highlights and shading to the image with colored pencils. Use mineral spirits and blending stumps to blend colors.

Using foam squares, attach Birthday Bears blossom and sentiments to card front as shown.

Tie a bow with remaining ribbon; trim ends. Referring to photo, adhere bow to card front. ✘

Sources: *Printed papers from BasicGrey; digital stamp from Sassy Cheryl's; colored pencils from Prismacolor; Copic markers from Imagination International Inc.; Word Window punch from Stampin' Up!; Effervescence border punch from Fiskars; die template from Spellbinders™ Paper Arts.*

Materials

- Card stock: brown metallic, light yellow, white, orange
- Sugar Rush double-sided printed papers: Orange Slices, Pulled Taffy
- Birthday Bears digital stamp
- Markers
- Colored pencils
- Yellow chalk
- Odorless mineral spirits
- Blending stumps
- Sandpaper pad
- 14 inches ⅝-inch-wide brown satin ribbon
- Punches: Word Window, Effervescence border
- Blossom die template (#S4-192)
- Die-cutting machine
- Adhesive foam squares
- Paper adhesive
- Computer with printer

True Friend

Design by **Kathy Menzies**

Form a 6 x 6-inch top-folded card from white card stock. Cut a 5⅞ x 5⅞-inch square of bronze metallic card stock; adhere to card front.

Cut a 5¾ x 5¾-inch square of Cordovan paper. Cut a 2⅛ x 5¾-inch strip of bronze metallic card stock; punch scallops along bottom edge. Cut a 2 x 5¾-inch strip of Woodrose paper; punch bottom edge with Deep Edger Garden Trellis punch. Adhere Woodrose strip on top of bronze metallic strip. Adhere to Cordovan square 2½ inches below top edge.

Wrap dark tan ribbon around square along top edge of scalloped strip; secure ribbon ends to back. Wrap a 10½-inch length of pink ribbon over dark tan ribbon; secure ends to back. Center and adhere square to card front. Tie a bow with remaining pink ribbon; trim ends; adhere to left side of card front as shown.

Stamp sentiment onto white card stock. Cut a rectangle around sentiment and round lower right corner. Adhere to bronze metallic card stock; trim a small border. Accent "friend" with pearls; adhere to lower right corner of card front.

Using computer and printer, print three copies of Mum Blossom image, printing each image on a separate piece of white card stock. Color one mum completely with colored pencils, blending colors with mineral spirits and blending stumps. In the same manner, color only the flower on second mum and only center of flower on third mum. Add glitter glue to center of third mum; let dry. Cut a 2½ x 3⅝-inch rectangle around first mum; round all four corners. Carefully trim around colored areas on second and third mums. Using foam tape, attach all three mum layers together. Adhere layered mum to dark pink card stock; trim a small border. Adhere to bronze metallic card stock with foam tape; trim a small border. Use foam tape to attach layered mum to card front. ✗

Sources: Card stock from Paper Temptress and Memory Box; Stardream metallic card stock from Gruppo Cordenons available from Paper Mojo; printed papers from BasicGrey; stamp set from Papertrey Ink; digital stamp from KLM Designs; colored pencils from Faber-Castell USA Inc.; Deep Edger Garden Trellis punch from Martha Stewart Crafts; Scallop Edger from Stampin' Up!; glitter glue from Ranger Industries Inc.

Materials

- Card stock: white, dark pink, bronze metallic
- Indian Summer printed papers: Cordovan, Woodrose
- In Bloom stamp set
- Mum Blossom digital stamp
- Red pigment ink pad
- Colored pencils: madder, dark red, olive green, yellow-green, gold, Pompeian red
- Odorless mineral spirits
- Blending stumps
- Sandpaper pad
- 2 self-adhesive red pearls
- Ribbons: 20 inches ⅞-inch-wide pink sheer, 10½ inches ½-inch-wide dark tan
- Punches: Deep Edger Garden Trellis, Scallop Edger, corner rounder
- Piercing tool
- Craft sponge
- Clear glitter glue
- Adhesive foam tape
- Paper adhesive
- Computer and printer

THERE'S NOTHING BETTER THAN A TRUE *friend*

Watercolor Techniques

Color has taken possession of me; no longer do I have to chase after it. I know that it has hold of me forever … Color and I are one. I am a painter.

—Paul Klee

The art of watercolor has been around for many years. The fundamental practice of mixing water with color and using it to bring images to life can be found in so many different forms. Artists and crafters have used paint pots, watercolor crayons, watercolor pencils, inks and dyes to apply color to a wide variety of surfaces using many different items to gather the pigment needed to paint with. The tools used to apply the color have varied from a simple paintbrush that needs to be dipped in water, to water brushes with barrels that can be filled with water to allow the user control over the amount of water being used while applying color. Each color medium and tool used produces a different end result.

In this book, we will be using watercolor pencils to demonstrate the basic technique of watercoloring. You will note the high vibrancy of color in our sample project. Although it may be more vibrant than you are accustomed to, you will be better able to see the technique in a step-by-step process. Because each medium and application of that medium will vary by user, you are encouraged to practice, practice, practice.

Aside from the actual color medium and tool used to apply that medium, there are a few other items that you need before you get started. First you will need a waterproof ink that will not run or feather when it gets wet. There are many inks on the market that are suitable for this type of work—some are solvent-based, some are pigment-based. It is best to stay away from water-based dye inks as they tend to be unstable, and while it may not run in one section of your watercoloring, you may find it highly distressing to see it begin to feather and run just as you finish watercoloring your image. You will also need thick card stock or watercolor paper. Watercolor paper is known by its rough or "toothy" texture and will help give your project an authentic watercolor look. It is this texture that also allows the paper to capture pigment and water without causing the paper to pucker or curl.

One last highly useful item is a palette of sorts to test the true color that you will be working with, or to mix colors to get the color exactly to your liking. A simple yet wonderful palette is a scrap of the same paper you plan on using for your project. That way, when testing color, you can also get a feel for the flow of your colors. It is also useful when you need to remove excess water from your brush or just to have better control of the amount of color being applied to your image.

Now that we have covered the basic supplies needed and have explained why you are using these items, you are invited to follow along step-by-step to learn exactly how to use these tools to bring your stamped images to life.

Gather supplies including watercolor pencils, a watercolor brush or water brush, a small jar of water and a scrap piece of paper to use as a palette.

1. Stamp your image onto watercolor paper.

2. Begin by lightly outlining each stem and leaf with a light green watercolor pencil. Moisten just the tip of the watercolor brush and gently blend the color into the open areas of the stems and leaves.

3. At the base near the grass, moisten the brush once again and gently blend the color from the grass areas, drawing the watercolor brush to the edges of the paper. Use water sparingly at this point, only remoistening the tip of your brush as needed to blend and drag the color.

4. Add additional colors to the base of the grass area using small light strokes, blending as shown before, using just a bit more water than the first time. Apply color sparingly, as you can always layer in more color, but it can be hard to remove color or keep it just where you intend it to be when using water as your blending agent.

5. Add a thicker line of color around the outside of the flower centers. Wet your brush; wiggle the tip of the paintbrush in the color and drag the color outward toward the tip of each petal. The color will wash lightly out to the end of the petals.

6. Add color to the centers of the flowers, this time taking care to apply it to the bottom left of each center and petals of the smaller flowers. Applying color in this way will begin to start the shading of your image. It will cause the image to appear as if there is a light source in the top right corner of your image. Blend the color up toward the top right of each section.

7. Apply color to the rest of the bug image, applying it more heavily to the left. Using a wet brush tip as before, wiggle and drag the color into the open area, making sure to leave some areas much lighter than others, to give good contrast and shading.

8. Once you have applied all of the color you desire, you should have an image that looks similar to this one.

9. Scribble a small "puddle" of black and white onto your scrap paper palette. Drip a small portion of water into the color and begin to blend the colors together. Apply the color first directly from the palette to the left side of the wing and drag it to the top right.

10. As a finishing touch, add a bit of shadow beneath the largest flower and to the top surface of the left side of the grass. This gives the image the appearance of a shadow cast from the "light source" at the top right of the image. Use your watercolored image to create your finished project.

Hap-bee Day

Design by **Keri Lee Sereika**

Form a 7 x 5-inch top-folded card from orange card stock.

Cut a 6¾ x 4¾-inch piece of red card stock. Cut a 6⅝ x 2¼-inch piece of Lounging paper and a 6⅝ x 2½-inch piece of Glimmer paper; adhere to red card stock as shown. Adhere a 6⅝ x ⅝-inch strip of yellow card stock over paper seam. Wrap ribbon around yellow strip as shown; tie a bow; trim ends. Adhere rectangle centered to card front.

Die-cut a 2⅝ x 3⅜-inch rectangle from watercolor paper. Stamp Mr. Bumbly's Daisy onto rectangle; color using watercolor pencils. Outline image with watercolor pencils as shown, using a watercolor brush to blend colors.

Die-cut a 2⅞ x 3¾-inch scalloped rectangle from red card stock. Adhere watercolor rectangle onto scalloped rectangle. Pierce a hole in each corner of watercolor rectangle; attach brads. Using foam squares, attach rectangle to card front as shown.

Stamp "Hap-bee Day!" onto watercolor paper. Die-cut sentiment with 2½ x ½-inch Double Ended Tag die. Pierce a hole through each end of tag; insert brads. Adhere to lower right corner of card front. ✘

Sources: Card stock from Bazzill Basics Paper Inc.; printed paper from Fancy Pants Designs; stamps from Inky Antics; die templates from Spellbinders™ Paper Arts.

Materials

- Watercolor paper
- Card stock: orange, red, yellow
- Summer Soiree double-sided printed papers: Lounging, Glimmer
- Stamps: Mr. Bumbly's Daisy, Hap-bee Day
- Black solvent ink pad
- Watercolor pencils
- 6 small bronze brads
- 22 inches ½-inch-wide yellow grosgrain ribbon
- Die templates: Double Ended Tag (#S3-149), Classic Rectangles SM (#S4-130), Classic Scalloped Rectangles SM (#S4-133)
- Die-cutting machine
- Watercolor brush
- Piercing tool
- Adhesive foam squares
- Paper adhesive

Duet Hi

Design by **Broni Holcombe**

Form a 5 x 5-inch top-folded card from kraft card stock. Cut a 4¾ x 3⅞-inch piece of aqua card stock and a 4¾ x 1½-inch piece of yellow dot paper. Adhere yellow dot piece to aqua piece aligning bottom edges.

Cut a 4⅛ x 2⅛-inch piece of red dot paper. Trim top, bottom and right edges with pinking shears. Adhere to yellow/aqua piece ⅝ inch from bottom edge, aligning left edges. Wrap ribbon around layered piece over seam; secure ends to back. Adhere to card front as shown.

Stamp image onto watercolor paper. Color image by painting over area with wet watercolor brush, followed by reinkers. Use one reinker color at a time; let dry completely. Die-cut a 2⅜-inch circle around image. Die-cut a 3¼-inch dahlia from cork sheet. Adhere stamped circle on top of cork dahlia. Using foam tape, attach to card front as shown.

Attach "HI!" stickers onto lower right corner of card front. ✘

Sources: Watercolor paper and dye reinkers from Stampin' Up!; card stock from Papertrey Ink; Early Bird Mini Deck Paper Pad from Cosmo Cricket; stamp from Inkadinkado; archival ink pad from Ranger Industries Inc.; alphabet stickers from American Crafts Inc.; die templates from Spellbinders™ Paper Arts.

Materials

- Watercolor paper
- Card stock: kraft, aqua
- Early Bird Mini Deck Paper Pad
- Self-adhesive cork sheet
- Duet stamp
- Black archival ink pad
- Dye reinkers: real red, kiwi kiss, crushed curry, soft sky
- Aqua alphabet stickers
- 6 inches ⅝-inch-wide red/white-stitch ribbon
- Die templates: Standard Circles LG (#S4-114), Dahlia (#S4-191)
- Die-cutting machine
- Watercolor brush
- Pinking shears
- Adhesive foam tape
- Paper adhesive

Shopping Granny

Design by **Broni Holcombe**

Form a 4¼ x 5½-inch side-folded card from teal card stock. Cut a 4 x 5¼-inch rectangle of brown card stock. Cut a 3¾ x 2⅞-inch piece of red printed paper and a 3¾ x 2¹⁄₁₆-inch piece of yellow printed paper. Adhere pieces to brown rectangle as shown. Using sewing machine, zigzag-stitch around edge of brown rectangle and printed papers. Wrap ribbon around bottom of rectangle ¾ inch from bottom edge; tie a bow; trim ends. Layer crocheted flowers; attach brad; adhere to bow.

Die-cut a 3⅝-inch label from teal card stock. Cut a 3 x 3-inch square from brown card stock; adhere to teal label.

Using fine-detail ink, stamp shopping granny image onto watercolor paper. Color image by painting over area with wet watercolor brush, followed by reinkers. Use one reinker color at a time; let dry completely. Die-cut a 3¼-inch circle around image. Adhere centered to layered label. Using foam tape, attach to card front as shown.

Stamp sentiment onto watercolor paper using archival ink. Die-cut a 2 x ⅞-inch oval around words. Die-cut a 2¼ x 1⅛-inch oval from teal card stock. Adhere stamped oval to teal oval. Adhere to lower right area of card front. ✗

Sources: Card stock and dye reinkers from Stampin' Up!; Material Girl Mini Deck Paper Pad from Cosmo Cricket; stamp set from Our Craft Lounge; archival ink pad from Ranger Industries Inc.; fine-detail ink pad from Tsukineko LLC; die templates from Spellbinders™ Paper Arts.

Materials

- Watercolor paper
- Card stock: brown, teal
- Material Girl Mini Deck Paper Pad
- Shop 'Til Ya Flop stamp set
- Black ink pads: archival, fine-detail
- Dye reinkers: blush blossom, dusty Durango, real red, crushed curry, Bermuda bay, kiwi kiss, soft suede, going grey
- 18 inches ½-inch-wide brown/white-dot grosgrain ribbon
- Crocheted flowers: large cream, small teal
- Pink brad
- Die templates: Standard Circles LG (#S4-114), Labels Three (#S4-189), Petite Ovals SM (S4-140), Petite Ovals LG (S4-138)
- Die-cutting machine
- Sewing machine with brown thread
- Watercolor brush
- Adhesive foam tape
- Paper adhesive

Warm Fuzzies

Design by **Trudy Sjolander**

Materials

- Card stock: white, dark brown
- Swiss Dot Mud Puddle textured card stock
- Granola double-sided printed papers: Sunflower, Crunchy, Honey, Flax
- Puppy Love stamp
- Black solvent ink pad
- 24-color watercolor set
- Clear embossing liquid
- 16 inches ⅝-inch-wide gold ribbon
- Thread: brown, blue
- 8 black large round brads
- Classic Rectangles SM die template (#S4-130)
- Die-cutting machine
- Watercolor brush
- Piercing tool
- Sewing machine
- Adhesive foam tape
- Paper adhesive

Form a 6 x 6-inch top-folded card from textured card stock.

Cut a 5¼ x 5¼-inch square from Crunchy paper, adhere to dark brown card stock; trim a small border. Using sewing machine and blue thread, zigzag-stitch along edge of Crunchy square. Pierce a hole through each corner of Crunchy square; attach brads. Wrap an 8-inch length of ribbon vertically around square as shown. Secure ends to back. Adhere square to card front as shown.

Cut a 5¼ x 1½-inch strip from Sunflower paper, a 5⅝ x 2-inch strip of Flax paper and a 6 x 2¼-inch strip of dark brown card stock. Layer and adhere strips together. Zigzag-stitch along outer edge of Sunflower strip with brown thread. Wrap an 8-inch length of ribbon around layered strip as shown securing ends to back. Using foam tape, attach strip centered to card.

Die-cut a 3⅜ x 2⅝-inch rectangle from white card

stock. Stamp Puppy Love onto rectangle. Stamp a second image onto a scrap piece of white card stock. Using watercolors and watercolor brush, color both images and area below image on die-cut rectangle. Cut out dog's face and cat held in dog's arms from image on scrap card stock. Add clear embossing liquid to dog's nose; let dry completely. Using foam tape, attach to die-cut image as shown.

Adhere die-cut rectangle to a piece of Flax paper; trim a small border. Adhere to Honey paper; trim a small border. Adhere to dark brown card stock; trim a small border. Zigzag-stitch along edge of Honey rectangle with blue thread. Straight-stitch around edge of Flax rectangle with brown thread. Pierce a hole through each corner of die-cut rectangle; attach brads. Using a double layer of foam tape, attach to card front as shown. ✗

Sources: Card stock from Neenah Paper Inc. and Bazzill Basics Paper Inc.; textured card stock from Bazzill Basics Paper Inc.; printed paper from BasicGrey; stamp from Inky Antics; watercolor set from Koh-I-Noor; Crystal Effects embossing liquid from Stampin' Up!; die template from Spellbinders™ Paper Arts.

Thank You Butterflies

Design by **Debbie Olson**

Form a 5 x 7-inch side-folded card from cream card stock.

Adhere a 4¾ x 6¾-inch piece of Collector's Item paper to light orange card stock; trim a small border. Using sewing machine, straight-stitch around edge of Collector's Item paper. Cut two 4¾ x 1⅛-inch strips of Still in Box paper. Adhere strips to card front as shown. Using sewing machine, straight-stitch top edges and zigzag-stitch bottom edges of strips.

Cut a 3¼ x 5⅛-inch rectangle from watercolor paper. Line edges of rectangle with masking tape. Using black ink, stamp Antique Writing background onto watercolor rectangle. Re-ink stamp; stamp image onto another piece of watercolor paper. Remove masking tape from rectangle. Watercolor stamped rectangle with watercolor crayons. Color two of the butterflies on second stamped image in the same manner; let dry completely. Cut out butterflies. Attach teal gems to larger cut-out butterfly. Accent butterflies with glitter pens as desired. Using multiple layers of foam tape, attach cut-out butterflies to butterflies on rectangle as shown.

Using Horizontal Slot punch, punch a slot through butterfly rectangle 1 inch from bottom edge and ½ inch from right edge. Thread a 7-inch length of ribbon through slot; wrap ribbon around layered paper rectangle; secure ends of ribbon to back. Using foam tape, secure butterfly rectangle to card front as shown. Adhere ribbon-wrapped rectangle to card front.

Die-cut a 2¼ x ½-inch tag from cream card stock, cut off one end; ink edges light brown. Using turquoise ink, stamp "thank you" onto tag. Insert string through tag hole. Adhere string to card front over punched slot; secure tag with foam tape.

Tie a bow with remaining ribbon; trim ends. Adhere bow to card front over punched slot and string. ✘

Sources: Printed papers from October Afternoon; stamps from Hero Arts; solvent ink pad and chalk pigment ink from Tsukineko LLC; watercolor crayons and punch from Stampin' Up!; Spica glitter pens from Imagination International Inc.; die template from Spellbinders™ Paper Arts.

Materials

- Watercolor paper
- Card stock: light orange, cream
- The Thrift Shop double-sided printed papers: Still in Box, Collector's Item
- Stamps: Antique Writing background, Mi Casa set
- Ink pads: black solvent, turquoise chalk pigment, light brown dye
- Watercolor crayons
- Glitter pens: clear, light yellow
- 18 inches ⅝-inch-wide light orange ribbon
- 3½ inches natural string
- 4 self-adhesive teal gems
- Double Ended Tags die template (#S3-149)
- Die-cutting machine
- Horizontal Slot punch
- Watercolor brushes: large, small
- Sewing machine with cream thread
- Masking tape
- Adhesive foam tape
- Paper adhesive

Chickadee

Design by **Dawn Lusk**

Form a 4¼ x 5⅜-inch side-folded card from white card stock.

Using embossing machine and embossing folder, emboss a 4 x 5⅛-inch piece of white card stock. Adhere embossed piece to blue-gray card stock; trim a small border. Adhere to card front as shown.

Using Petite Ovals SM die template, die-cut a 4⁵⁄₁₆ x 3³⁄₁₆-inch oval from white card stock. Stamp chickadee image onto oval. Color image using reinkers; wet watercolor brush before applying reinker to dilute colors; blend colors while inks are still wet. Let dry completely. To color background of oval, lightly wet area with watercolor brush before coloring with reinkers. Let dry completely. Detail berries using gel pen. Using stamp positioner, restamp image with black ink.

Using Petite Ovals LG die template, die-cut a 4⅝ x 3½-inch oval from blue-gray card stock. Adhere stamped oval to blue-gray oval. Adhere layered oval centered to card front. ✗

Sources: Card stock from Bazzill Basics Paper Inc.; stamp set from Our Daily Bread designs; reinkers from Ranger Industries Inc.; gel pen from Sakura of America; die templates from Spellbinders™ Paper Arts; Cuttlebug die-cutting and embossing machine, and embossing folder from Provo Craft; stamp positioner from EK Success.

Materials

- Card stock: white, blue-gray
- You Will Find Refuge stamp set
- Black dye ink pad
- Dye reinkers: slate, cranberry, ginger, rust, latte, espresso, denim
- White gel pen
- Die templates: Petite Ovals LG (#S4-138), Petite Ovals SM (#S4-140)
- Victoria embossing folder (#37-1916)
- Die-cutting and embossing machine
- Stamp positioner
- Watercolor brush
- Paper adhesive

Tender Thoughts

Design by **Dawn Lusk**

Form a 4 x 7-inch side-folded card from light blue card stock. Using embossing machine and embossing folder, emboss a row of dots on card front ½ inch from bottom edge. In the same manner, emboss another row of dots on reverse side of card front ¼ inch from bottom edge.

Stamp three large daisies and three small daisies onto sticky notes, creating daisy masks. Carefully cut out flowers; set aside.

Cut a 3 x 6-inch rectangle of white card stock. Stamp two large daisies onto white rectangle as shown; attach daisy masks to first two daisies. Turn rectangle slightly to produce a more natural look before stamping each new flower. Stamp third large daisy slightly overlapping first large daisy. Mask remaining daisy. Stamp three small daisies onto rectangle as desired, masking when needed. Remove all masks; color daisies using reinkers, blending colors with watercolor brush while inks are still wet; let dry completely. Add detail to center of flowers with gel pen.

Mask all daisies. Apply green reinkers to background foliage stamp. Stamp over masked daisies. Let dry completely; remove masks.

Using stamp positioner, restamp all daisies with black ink. Stamp "Tender Thoughts" onto upper left corner of white rectangle with black ink; tear off bottom edge of rectangle. Cut a 3⅛ x 6-inch piece of black card stock; tear off bottom edge. Adhere stamped rectangle to black card stock. Cut a 3½ x 6½-inch piece of lavender card stock; tear off bottom edge. Adhere layered rectangle to lavender card stock.

Cut a 4½-inch length of ribbon. Wrap ribbon around bottom of layered rectangle; secure ends to back. Tie a three-loop bow with remaining ribbon; trim ends. Using adhesive dots, attach bow to rectangle as shown. Adhere rectangle to card front as shown. ✘

Sources: Card stock from Bazzill Basics Paper Inc.; stamp sets from Innovative Stamp Creations Inc.; reinkers from Ranger Industries Inc.; gel pen from Sakura of America; Cuttlebug embossing machine and folder from Provo Craft; stamp positioner from EK Success.

Materials

- Card stock: white, light blue, lavender, black
- Sticky notes
- Stamp sets: Dainty Daisies, Natures Silhouettes
- Black dye ink pad
- Dye reinkers: butterscotch, wild plum, eggplant, peeled paint, shabby shutters
- White gel pen
- 28 inches ¼-inch-wide black/white checked ribbon
- Border With Love embossing folder (#37-1171)
- Embossing machine
- Stamp positioner
- Watercolor brush
- Adhesive dots
- Paper adhesive

Materials

- Watercolor paper
- Card stock: brown, white textured
- Origins Sugar Pea printed paper
- Stamp sets: Whispy Blooms, Blooming Expressions
- Ink pads: black archival, brown dye
- Dye reinkers: barely banana, crushed curry, wild wasabi, soft suede
- 3 small brown buttons
- 9 inches ⅝-inch-wide green grosgrain ribbon
- Floral Vine Deep Edge Punch
- Sewing machine with brown thread
- Watercolor brush
- Craft sponge
- Brown glitter glue
- Paper adhesive

Floral Trio

Design by **Broni Holcombe**

Form a 5½ x 4¼-inch top-folded card from brown card stock.

Cut a 5⅜ x 4⅛-inch rectangle of white card stock. Cut a 5¼ x 2½-inch piece of Sugar Pea paper; adhere to top of white rectangle, leaving a small border. Cut a 5¼ x 2½-inch piece of brown card stock; punch bottom edge with edge punch; adhere to white rectangle as shown. Cut a 5¼ x 1⅛-inch strip of white card stock; ink edges brown. Using brown ink, stamp "You are in my prayers" along upper right edge of strip. Adhere strip ⅛ inch from top of brown card-stock piece. Wrap ribbon over white strip; gather ribbon on right edge, secure ends to back. Using sewing machine, straight-stitch gathered ribbon. Adhere to card front as shown.

Using black ink, stamp four flowers and four leaves onto watercolor paper. Color flowers and leaves using dye reinkers; let dry completely. Cut out images. Wet backs of cut pieces; bend and form with fingers to curve petals and leaves. Adhere to card front as shown, layering two of the flowers. Accent flower centers with glitter glue. Adhere buttons to flowers as shown. ✗

Sources: *Watercolor paper, brown card stock and dye reinkers from Stampin' Up!; white textured card stock from Couture Cardstock; printed paper from BasicGrey; Whispy Blooms stamp set from Our Craft Lounge; Blooming Expressions stamp set from Whipper Snapper Designs Inc.; archival ink pad and glitter glue from Ranger Industries Inc.; edge punch from Martha Stewart Crafts.*

Thank You

Design by **Jeanne Streiff**

Form a 5 x 5-inch top-folded card from black card stock.

Cut a 4¾ x 4¾-inch square from light brown card stock. Using brown ink, stamp swirls along left edge of brown square. Adhere centered to card front.

Cut a 3½ x 3½-inch square from white card stock. Using black ink, stamp "Thank You" sentiments at center bottom of white square. Use markers to color flowers and top "Thank You" as shown. Sponge edges brown. Adhere stamped square to black card stock; trim a small border. Adhere to card front as shown.

Stamp three flowers onto watercolor paper using black ink. Using watercolor paint and watercolor brush, paint flowers. Let dry completely. Apply Flower Soft Glue to center of each flower; add brown sprinkles. Adhere flowers to card front as shown, applying adhesive to centers of flower backs only. ✗

Sources: *Card stock from Couture Cardstock; stamp sets from Our Craft Lounge; solvent ink pad from Tsukineko LLC; watercolor by Salis International Inc.; Copic markers from Imagination International Inc.; sprinkles and Flower Soft Glue from Flower Soft Inc.*

Materials

- Watercolor paper
- Card stock: light brown, black, white
- Stamp sets: Whispy Blooms, Whispy Patterns
- Ink pads: black solvent, brown dye
- Red watercolor paint
- Alcohol-based-ink markers: brick beige, light rouge
- Brown sprinkles
- Watercolor brush
- Craft sponge
- Flower Soft Glue
- Paper adhesive

We Heard the Buzzzz

Design by **Trudy Sjolander**

Form a 5½ x 5½-inch top-folded card from white card stock.

Cut a 4¾ x 4¾-inch square from Peanut Brittle paper. Adhere to Jaw Breakers paper; trim a small border. Using sewing machine, zigzag-stitch along edge of Peanut Brittle square. Wrap a 6-inch length of ribbon around layered square ¾ inch above bottom edge of Peanut Brittle square; wrap and secure ribbon ends to back. Tie a bow with remaining ribbon; trim ends; adhere centered on top of wrapped ribbon. Adhere layered square to card front as shown.

Die-cut a 3¾ x 2⅞-inch rectangle from white card stock. Stamp Bees onto rectangle. Stamp Bees image twice onto scrap pieces of white card stock. Using watercolors and watercolor brush, color all bees on die-cut rectangle and second set of bees. Paint a blue shadow around bees on die-cut rectangle. Color only the heads of bees on last set of bees. Let dry completely.

Using a clean watercolor brush, paint a layer of embossing liquid over heads of last set of bees; let dry completely. Cut out bees on second set of bees image, cutting off wings and antennae. Cut out heads on third set of bees, cutting off antennae.

On die-cut rectangle, detail bees' wings and antennae with glitter glue. Detail second set of bees' bodies and third set of bees' heads with glitter glue. Assemble bees' layers with foam tape as shown.

Adhere die-cut rectangle to Jaw Breakers paper; trim a small border. Adhere to Jelly Beans paper; trim a small border.

Punch four pointed petal flowers from Candy Hearts paper; trim two petals off each flower to create foliage for paper flowers. Place a paper flower on top of a punched flower and position it on one corner of layered bee rectangle; pierce a hole through center of flower going through all layers. Insert brad, securing flowers to rectangle. Repeat for each corner of bee rectangle. Using foam tape, adhere rectangle to card front as shown.

Adhere a 4⅝ x 4⅝-inch square of white card stock to Jelly Beans paper; trim a small border. Cut a 4⅛ x ⅞-inch strip of Jaw Breakers paper; adhere to bottom edge of white square. Cut a 4⅛ x ¾-inch strip of

Peanut Brittle paper; adhere to bottom edge of Jaw Breakers strip. Zigzag-stitch around outer edge of white square.

Hand-print, or use a computer to generate, "We heard the buzzzz…" onto white card stock. Cut a rectangle around sentiment; adhere to Jaw Breakers paper; trim a small border. Adhere to top of white square. Adhere layered square inside card. ✗

Sources: Card stock from Neenah Paper Inc.; printed papers from BasicGrey; stamp from Janlynn Corp./Stamps Happen Inc.; watercolor set from Koh-I-Noor; paper flowers from Prima Marketing Inc.; die template from Spellbinders™ Paper Arts.; punch from McGill Inc.; Crystal Effects embossing liquid from Stampin' Up!

Materials

- White card stock
- Sugar Rush double-sided printed papers: Jaw Breakers, Jelly Beans, Peanut Brittle, Candy Hearts
- Bees stamp
- Black solvent ink pad
- Black fine-tip pen
- 24-color watercolor set
- 13 inches ⅝-inch-wide lavender/white-dot sheer ribbon
- 4 lavender small paper flowers
- 4 orange small round brads
- Classic Rectangles LG die templates (#S4-132)
- Die-cutting machine
- Baby Blooms Perfect Petals Stacking Punch
- Watercolor brushes
- Piercing tool
- Sewing machine with blue thread
- Clear embossing liquid
- Glitter glue: clear, black, orange, yellow, clear iridescent
- Adhesive foam tape
- Paper adhesive
- Computer and printer (optional)

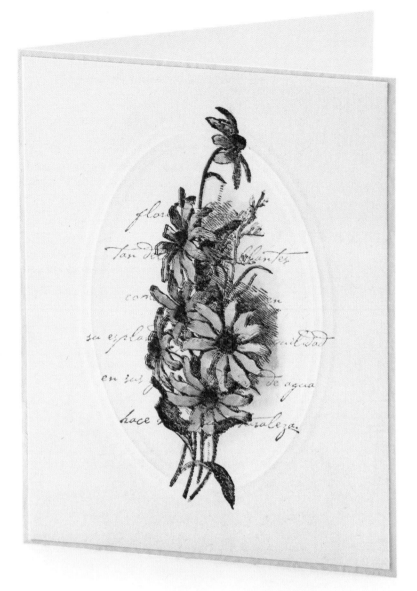

For You

Design by **Dawn Lusk**

Form a 3¾ x 4¾-inch side-folded card from light aqua card stock.

Cut a 3⅝ x 4⅝-inch rectangle from cream card stock. Using black ink, stamp script image onto scrap paper before stamping onto center of cream rectangle. Stamp floral image over script image as shown. Color floral image using reinkers, blending colors with watercolor brush while inks are still wet; let dry completely. Detail foliage with gel pen. Using stamp positioner, restamp floral image with black ink.

Using Classic Ovals LG die template and embossing machine, emboss an oval around stamped image. Adhere cream rectangle centered to card front. ✗

Sources: Card stock from Bazzill Basics Paper Inc.; stamp sets from Innovative Stamp Creations Inc.; reinkers from Ranger Industries Inc.; gel pen from Sakura of America; embossing machine and die templates from Spellbinders™ Paper Art; stamp positioner from EK Success.

Materials

- Card stock: light aqua, cream
- Scrap paper
- Beautiful Flowers stamp set
- Black dye ink pad
- Dye reinkers: butterscotch, rust, terra cotta, lettuce, bottle
- White gel pen
- Classic Ovals LG die template (#S4-110)
- Embossing machine
- Stamp positioner
- Watercolor brush
- Paper adhesive

Heartfelt Sympathy

Design by **Trudy Sjolander**

Form a 6 x 6-inch top-folded card from white striped card stock.

Cut a 5¼ x 5¼-inch square of white striped card stock. Adhere to lavender card stock; trim a border. Using sewing machine, zigzag-stitch along edge of white striped square.

Stamp Hummingbird with Flowers onto a 4⅛ x 4¼-inch piece of white card stock. Using watercolors and watercolor brush, color image; dilute and mix watercolors as desired. Let dry completely. Using a clean watercolor brush, detail leaves with clear embossing liquid; let dry completely.

Stamp sentiment on upper left corner on stamped square. Adhere to green card stock; trim a small border. Using foam tape, attach layered square to upper left area of stitched layered square.

Wrap a 5-inch length of ribbon around lower right corner of layered square as shown; secure ends to back. Tie a bow with remaining ribbon; trim ends. Adhere bow to wrapped ribbon as shown.

Adhere layered square centered to card front. Attach gems and pearls to card front as shown. ✗

Sources: Pearlescent card stock from Paper Temptress; Hummingbird with Flowers stamp from Inkadinkado; Heartfelt Sentiments stamp set from Clear Dollar Stamps; solvent ink pad from Tsukineko LLC; watercolor set from Koh-I-Noor; Crystal Effects embossing liquid from Stampin' Up!

Materials

- Pearlescent card stock: lavender, green, white, white striped
- Stamps: Hummingbird with Flowers, Heartfelt Sentiments set
- Black solvent ink pad
- 24-color watercolor set
- Clear embossing liquid
- 11 inches ⅜-inch-wide lavender sheer ribbon
- 3 light green small self-adhesive pearls
- Purple self-adhesive gems: 2 small, 2 medium, 2 large
- Scoring board
- Scoring tool
- Watercolor brushes
- Sewing machine with green thread
- Adhesive foam tape
- Paper adhesive

A Little Something

Design by **Trudy Sjolander**

Form a 4¾ x 4¾-inch top-folded card from white card stock.

Cut a 4¼ x 4¼-inch square from printed paper; adhere to light blue iridescent card stock; trim a small border. Using sewing machine, zigzag-stitch along edges of printed paper square.

Cut a 3¼ x 3¼-inch square of printed paper; adhere to light blue iridescent card stock; trim a small border. Adhere to white card stock; trim a small border. Straight-stitch around edge of printed paper using sewing machine. Using foam tape, attach small layered square centered to large layered square.

Wrap ribbon around layered squares as shown; secure ends to back. Adhere to card front as shown.

Die-cut a 2¾ x 2⅛-inch rectangle from white card stock and a 3¹⁄₁₆ x 2⅜-inch rectangle from light blue iridescent card stock. Using black ink, stamp turtle image once onto white die-cut rectangle and twice on scrap pieces of white card stock. Using watercolors and brush, color outer edge of turtle on die-cut rectangle. In the same manner, color entire turtle on second stamped image and only the balloon and flower on third stamped image. Let dry completely.

Using a clean watercolor brush, paint a layer of watermark ink onto shell of completely colored turtle. Apply ultra-thick embossing powder; emboss using embossing heat tool. Repeat process on colored balloon.

Detail balloon and center of colored flower with turquoise glitter glue. In the same manner, apply pink glitter glue to flower petals. Detail entirely colored turtle with lime green glitter glue as desired.

Cut out colored balloon, flower and turtle images from scrap paper. Using foam tape, attach turtle layers together as shown. Adhere turtle rectangle to light blue iridescent die-cut rectangle. In the same manner, attach to card front as shown.

Using black ink, stamp sentiment onto white card stock; trim to a 1¾ x ⅝-inch rectangle; V-notch right end. Ink edges mauve. Adhere to turquoise glitter card stock; trim a small border. Pierce a hole through lower left corner and attach olive green brad. Adhere to card front as shown.

Adhere flat-back acrylic stones to card front as shown. ✘

Sources: *Card stock from Paper Temptress, Neenah Paper Inc. and Hobby Lobby Stores Inc./The Paper Studio; printed paper from BasicGrey; Turtle's Balloon stamp from Inky Antics; Heartfelt Sentiments stamp set from Clear Dollar Stamps; chalk pigment ink pad and watermark ink refill from Tsukineko LLC; watercolor set from Koh-I-Noor; ultra-thick embossing powder and glitter glue from Ranger Industries Inc.; Dew Drops acrylic stones from The Robin's Nest; die templates from Spellbinders™ Paper Arts.*

Materials

- Card stock: white, light blue iridescent, turquoise glitter
- Sugar Shack Candy Hearts double-sided printed paper
- Stamps: Turtle's Balloon, Heartfelt Sentiments set
- Ink pads: black solvent, mauve chalk pigment
- Watermark ink refill
- 24-piece watercolor set
- Clear ultra-thick embossing powder
- 6 inches ⅝-inch-wide blue striped ribbon
- Olive green round brad
- 3 blue flat-back acrylic stones
- Die templates: Classic Rectangles SM (#S4-130), Classic Rectangles LG (#S4-132)
- Die-cutting machine
- Watercolor brushes
- Piercing tool
- Embossing heat tool
- Sewing machine with white thread
- Glitter glue: turquoise, pink, lime green
- Adhesive foam tape
- Paper adhesive

Secret Fishing Spot

Design by **Kathy Menzies**

Form a 6 x 6-inch top-folded card from white card stock.

Cut a 5⅝ x 5⅝-inch square of aqua card stock. Using brayer, apply white pigment ink to Cover-a-Card Flourishes stamp; stamp onto aqua square. Let dry completely. Ink brayer with aqua dye; roll over stamped square, repeat until square is evenly covered with color. Adhere to light moss green card stock; trim a small border. Adhere centered to card front.

Cut a 5⅝ x 2-inch strip of white card stock. Punch bottom edge with Iron Gate punch. Turn punched strip over and use scoring board and scoring tool to score two lines ⅛ inch apart on top edge. Wrap an 8½-inch length of aqua ribbon around white strip; secure ends to back with double-sided tape. Wrap an 8½-inch length of light moss green ribbon over aqua ribbon; secure ends in the same manner. Adhere to card front 1¼ inches from bottom edge.

Using brown ink, stamp Fishing Hole onto a 3¼ x 4⅝-inch piece of watercolor paper. Using reinkers and watercolor brush, color image starting at bottom, using water to blend colors as needed. To color sky and grass areas, lightly wet paper before applying reinker. Let dry completely. Once dry, use gel pen to add reflection lines to water and details to other parts of image as desired. Adhere to light aqua card stock; trim a small border. Using two layers of foam tape, attach to left side of card front.

Using Modern Label punch, punch a label from light moss green card stock. Using aqua ink, stamp "Thank You" onto white card stock. Punch stamped area with Word Window punch; attach to aqua label with foam tape. Place pearls on both ends of aqua label. Adhere to bottom of Fishing Hole image.

Cut a 1¾-inch length of light moss green ribbon and a 2½-inch length of aqua ribbon; V-notch ends. Create a bow by layering ribbons as shown. String button with thread; wrap thread around middle of layered ribbons; tie a knot and trim ends. Using double-sided tape, attach bow over right side of ribbon as shown. ✗

Sources: *Card stock from Paper Temptress and Papertrey Ink; stamps from Impression Obsession Inc.; distressed reinkers and gel pen from Ranger Industries Inc.; Iron Gate Edge punch from Martha Stewart Crafts; Word Window punch and Modern Label punch from Stampin' Up!*

Materials

- Watercolor paper
- Card stock: white, aqua, light aqua, light moss green
- Stamps: Fishing Hole, Cover-a-Card Flourishes, Sentiments II set
- Dye ink pads: brown, aqua
- White pigment ink pad
- Distressed reinkers: stormy sky, barn door, forest moss, crushed olive, weathered wood, vintage photo, walnut satin
- White gel pen
- Light moss green button
- 2 self-adhesive green pearls
- Ribbon: 11 inches ⅞-inch-wide aqua grosgrain, 11 inches ⅜-inch-wide light moss green twill
- White thread
- Punches: Iron Gate Edge, Word Window, Modern Label
- Scoring board
- Scoring tool
- Brayer
- Watercolor brush
- Double-sided tape
- Adhesive foam tape
- Paper adhesive

THANK YOU

Stargazer Lilies

Design by **Christine Okken**

Form a 5½ x 4¼-inch top-folded card from bright pink card stock.

Cut a 5⅜ x 4⅛-inch rectangle from shimmery white card stock. Turn rectangle over and score a vertical line ⅜ inch from right edge; turn rectangle over. The scored line will now be on the left side. Attach a 4½-inch length of ¼-inch-wide double-sided tape to rectangle ¼ inch to the right of scored line. Apply glitter to tape; tap off extra with fingers. Using piercing template and tool, pierce a corner swirl design in upper right corner of rectangle. Adhere card stock centered to card front.

Cut a 5½ x 1-inch strip of bright pink card stock. Punch bottom edge with Round Lattice punch. Attach two 5½-inch lengths of ⅛-inch-wide double-sided tape to punched strip as shown. Apply glitter to tape; tap off extra with fingers. Adhere to bottom of shimmery white rectangle.

Die-cut a 3¾ x 2⅞-inch deckle-edge oval from bright pink card stock. Using foam squares, attach to card front as shown.

Using pink ink, stamp "Congratulations" onto shimmery white card stock. Punch out word with oval punch. Adhere to right edge of pink oval. Embellish with rhinestones.

Using black ink, stamp lily image twice onto watercolor paper. Color lilies using reinkers and watercolor brush, blending colors while inks are still wet. Let dry completely. Add more color to lilies using water-based markers, blending when needed with wet watercolor brush. Let dry completely and cut out. Using foam squares, attach lilies to card front as shown.

Tie a bow with ribbon; V-notch ends. Attach to card front as shown with adhesive dots. ✘

Sources: *Watercolor paper and stamp sets from Flourishes; card stock, reinkers and markers from Stampin' Up!; die template from Spellbinders™ Paper Arts; Round Lattice punch from Martha Stewart Crafts; piercing template and piercing tool from Ecstasy Crafts Inc.*

Materials

- Watercolor paper
- Card stock: bright pink, shimmery white
- Stamp sets: Lily of Hope, Tag Lines
- Ink pads: pink dye, black solvent
- Dye reinkers: pixie pink, pink passion, certainly celery
- Water-based markers: pixie pink, certainly celery, pumpkin pie, garden green
- Clear glitter
- 3 self-adhesive clear rhinestones
- 10 inches 1¼-inch-wide white silk ribbon
- Deckled Edge Classic Ovals Large die template (#S4-259)
- Die-cutting machine
- Punches: Round Lattice, oval
- Ornare Corner Stencil Piercing Template (#4055587)
- Piercing tool
- Scoring board
- Scoring tool
- Watercolor brush
- Double-sided tape: ⅛-inch-wide, ¼-inch-wide
- Adhesive dots
- Adhesive foam squares
- Paper adhesive

Vintage Christmas

Design by **Laurie Wilson**

Form a 5½ x 4¼-inch top-folded card from olive green card stock. Cut a 5¼ x 4-inch rectangle from cream floral paper; adhere to red card stock; trim a small border. Using sewing machine, stitch two curving lines around edge of printed paper.

Wrap olive green ribbon around layered rectangle as shown; secure ends to back. Wrap a 7½-inch length of red ribbon over olive green ribbon; secure ends to back. Tie a bow with remaining red ribbon; trim ends; set aside. Adhere rectangle centered to card front.

Using computer and printer, print three copies of Christmas Ornament Decorative Edge digital image onto watercolor paper. Use watercolor pencils to color images, blending colors with a wet watercolor brush as desired. Once dry, add details with pearlescent watercolors; let dry completely. Detail ornaments on one image with white gel pen. Spray detailed ornament image and second image lightly with acrylic sealer. Let dry completely.

Using a Standard Circles die template, trace a 3¼-inch circle around un-glossed image; do not trace over colored area. Cut out circle and around edges of image. Stamp "Merry Christmas" onto upper right side of circle. Sponge ink onto circle as desired. Adhere to red card stock; trim a small border. Adhere to olive green card stock; trim a small border. Machine-stitch along edges of stamped circle. Using foam squares, attach layered circle to card front as shown.

Cut remaining two colored images into layering pieces as desired. Use foam squares to stack and attach layers to card front as shown. Attach detailed ornaments last.

Attach red gems to both sides of "Merry." Adhere bow to card front as shown using adhesive dots. ✗

Sources: *Card stock pad from Papertrey Ink; digital stamp from KLM Designs; stamp set from Clear Dollar Stamps; watercolor pencils from Faber-Castell Inc.; pearlescent watercolor set from Yasutomo & Co.; die template from Spellbinders™ Paper Arts.*

Materials

- Watercolor paper
- Card stock: red, olive green
- Cream floral printed paper
- Christmas Ornament Decorative Edge digital stamp
- Holiday Nutcrackers stamp set
- Olive green dye ink pad
- Watercolor pencils: warm grey I, light yellow ochre, permanent carmine, olive green yellowish, Indian red
- 21-color pearlescent watercolor set
- White gel pen
- Ribbon: 7½ inches ⅝-inch-wide olive green grosgrain, 14 inches ½-inch-wide red satin
- 2 red small self-adhesive gems
- Standard Circles LG die template (#S4-114)
- Watercolor brush
- Craft sponge
- Sewing machine with dark cream thread
- Spray bottle
- Acrylic high-gloss sealer spray
- Adhesive foam squares
- Adhesive dots
- Paper adhesive
- Computer with printer

Merry
CHRISTMAS

Marker Techniques

My skin is kind of sort of brownish pinkish yellowish white.
My eyes are grayish bluish green, but i'm told they look orange in the night.
My hair is reddish blondish brown, but it's silver when it's wet,
And all the colors I am inside have not been invented yet.

—Shel Silverstein

Right now one of the hottest trends in coloring stamped images is, of course, using alcohol-based-ink markers. These markers are available from various manufacturers in a wide range of qualities and an even wider range of colors. One of the main reasons that these markers are so highly popular is their ability to blend colors or shades of colors without leaving telltale lines. Many manufacturers market a colorless blender, but it is rarely used to blend colors. More often, it is used to remove color and fix errors. Blending is most often done by using a similar color that is either a few shades lighter than the color you are hoping to blend or is the lightest shade you started with on your project. This is why there are so many benefits to using markers from a manufacturer who offers a large variety of color choices. While the samples in this book are created using high-quality, artist-grade markers, don't hesitate to try the techniques as shown, using whatever alcohol-based-ink markers you may have. The end results may vary slightly, but the techniques taught can be applied and used with any type of alcohol markers.

Along with alcohol-based-ink markers, you will also need two other items, a nonsolvent-based ink pad and smooth-surface card stock, before practicing these techniques. A high-quality, dye-based detail ink will allow you to stamp a crisp, clean impression that will dry quickly without the use of a heat tool to fully set it. A good smooth-surfaced card stock with tightly woven fibers is also key in the ability to blend colors, as well as remove color as shown in various samples in this book. Because the ink formula in alcohol-based-ink markers can affect the ink of the stamped image, causing it to bleed, run or smudge while being colored, take time to test the inks you have on the card stock you plan to use before you begin your project.

1. Begin by stamping your image of choice onto smooth card stock. Allow ink to dry completely before coloring image. ***Note:*** *If you are just beginning, sometimes learning on a shaded image such as the one shown here will help you to know which colors to use where, further on in the shading portion of the steps. Here you can see that the "light" seems to be coming from the top right corner of the image as the shadows are to the left and across the bottom of the image.*

2. Once you have stamped your image, choose which colors you might need and have them all close at hand for easy selection during the coloring process.

3. Beginning with the lightest color you plan on using, color the entire area using small circular motions, being sure to fully saturate the card stock. Having a fully saturated image will help in blending additional colors as you add them.

4. Select a similar color in a slightly darker shade and begin to add depth by gently touching areas lightly with the tip of the marker. Blend by working with the first color using small circular motions.

5. Select your third color in the darkest shade and add more saturated color to the shadowed, or hash-marked areas to increase depth and shadowing. Once again, blend these colors by working with the first color using small circular motions. *Note: You can always add more color and repeat steps 4 and 5 until you achieve the desired look. It is better to repeat steps in adding color as it is much harder to remove too much or too dark of color once applied.*

6. As with the previous three steps, start by coloring the leaves with the lightest shade of green. Again, be sure to saturate the leaves completely for the best blending ability.

7. Because the leaves are so small, add additional levels of color using medium and dark shades until the desired look is achieved. Pay special attention to the shaded images to help you see where the lighter versus darker shading should be. Blend the leaves using the lightest shade of green that you used to begin with.

8. As a final step in bringing your image to life, add a bit of shading beneath the leaves and to the left of the total image. This gives your final image the grounding it needs to appear as though it is sitting on something rather than just floating in midair. If you find you have gone out of the lines in any area, simply "push the color" back into the lines using the colorless blender pen. Start outside the line and press the blender-pen tip to the paper and go right up to the outside edge of the line. Repeat until the color is fully removed and your image is how you want it to look. Now, all that is left to do is use your colored image on a finished project!

For the more advanced colorist: All of the steps will be the same when using a clear open-line art image, it will simply be up to you to determine the shading direction and application. A good tip to keep in mind would be to place an imaginary light source shining onto your image and imagine what it would look like if light were hitting from the same direction each time you add depth and shading. And again, remember that you can always add more color to increase the depth of your image, but it is very difficult to remove deep color once applied.

Pineapple Welcome

Design by **Keri Lee Sereika**

Form a 5 x 7-inch side-folded card from gray card stock.

Cut a 4⅝ x 6⅝-inch rectangle from light sage green card stock. Hand-print with black fine-tip marker, or use a computer to generate, "Welcome to the neighborhood" onto lower left area of rectangle. Stamp upper 4½ inches of rectangle with Cover-a-Card medallion using light brown ink. Cut a 4⅝ x ¾-inch strip of gray card stock; adhere to light sage green rectangle 2 inches from bottom edge. Wrap ribbon around rectangle over gray strip; tie in a bow; trim ends. Adhere rectangle to dark green card stock; trim a small border. Adhere centered to card front.

Using dark brown dye ink, stamp Pineapple onto white card stock. Use 3¾ x 3⅞-inch Labels Nine die template to die-cut a label around pineapple. Color pineapple with markers; add a shadow around pineapple. Using foam squares, adhere to center top of card front. Attach self-adhesive pearls to card front as shown. ✘

Sources: *Card stock from Bazzill Basics Paper Inc.; stamps from Impression Obession Inc.; chalk ink pad from Clearsnap Inc.; Copic markers from Imagination International Inc.; die-cutting machine and die templates from Spellbinders™ Paper Arts.*

Materials

- Card stock: gray, dark green, light sage green, white
- Stamps: Pineapple, Cover-a-Card Medallion
- Ink pads: dark brown dye, light brown chalk
- Alcohol-based-ink markers: black fine-tip, honey, buttercup yellow, golden yellow, pale sepia, yellow-green, Spanish olive, marine green, putty
- 15 inches ⅝-inch-wide brown satin ribbon
- Green self-adhesive pearls: 2 large, 2 medium
- Labels Nine die template (#S4-233)
- Die-cutting machine
- Adhesive foam squares
- Paper adhesive
- Computer with printer (optional)

Welcome
to the neighborhood

Materials

- Card stock: cream, red
- Early Bird Mini Deck paper pad
- Stamp sets: Beautiful Blossoms, Mega Mixed Messages
- Ink pads: dark brown, light brown, watermark
- Gold embossing powder
- Alcohol-based-ink markers: colorless blender, warm gray No. 00, warm gray No. 1, pale yellowish pink, light reddish yellow
- 9 inches ⅝-inch-wide moss green grosgrain ribbon
- 1 medium Brad Daddies with i-top Tool
- Tags Trio die template (#S3-148)
- Die-cutting machine
- Sewing machine with cream thread
- Embossing heat tool
- Piercing tool
- Craft sponge
- Adhesive foam tape
- Clear glitter glue
- Paper adhesive

Geranium Get Well

Design by **Debbie Olson**

Form a 4¼ x 5½-inch side-folded card from cream card stock.

Adhere a 2⅝ x 4¼-inch piece of red printed paper to a 4 x 5¼-inch piece of green printed paper. Machine-stitch around edge of red piece. Wrap ribbon around layered papers as shown, placing loose ends on right side.

Using dark brown ink, stamp "GET well" onto cream card stock. Die-cut sentiment with medium Tags Trio die template; ink edges light brown. Using i-top Tool and following manufacturer's instructions, wrap one medium Brad Daddies with red printed paper. Pierce a hole through ribbon and printed papers; attach brad with sentiment tag as shown.

Stamp geranium twice onto cream card stock using brown ink; color with markers. Color center of blooms darker and detail with glitter glue. Cut out geranium leaves and flowers to create layers as desired; set layers aside.

Using watermark ink, stamp germanium with border onto cream card stock; trim around outside border. Apply gold embossing powder to border; heat-emboss with embossing heat tool. Sponge border with light brown ink. Color outer edge of geranium with markers.

Using foam tape, attach layers to bordered geranium. In the same manner, attach oval to card front as shown. ✘

Sources: *Card stock and Mega Mixed Messages stamp set from Papertrey Ink; Early Bird Mini Deck paper pad from Cosmo Cricket; Beautiful Blossoms stamp set from JustRite; watermark ink pad from Tsukineko LLC; Copic markers from Imagination International Inc.; Brad Daddies and i-top Tool from Imaginisce; die template from Spellbinders™ Paper Arts; Stickles glitter glue from Ranger Industries Inc.*

Swing By Sometime

Design by **Christine Okken**

Form a 5½ x 4¼-inch top-folded card from dark red card stock.

Cut a 5⅜ x 4⅛-inch rectangle from olive green card stock. Cut a 5¼ x 1-inch strip from each printed paper; adhere to rectangle as shown. Straight-stitch around each strip using sewing machine.

Cut a 3⅝ x 3⅛-inch piece from cream card stock. Stamp tree with swing image onto cream piece. Color image with markers, using lighter colors first. Pierce two holes next to swing; attach brads. Adhere to dark red card stock; trim a small border. Straight-stitch around edge of cream piece. Punch a slit in upper right and lower left corners of image panel as shown. Cut ribbon into two lengths—a 3½-inch length and a 4-inch length. Run 3½-inch length of ribbon through top slit; adhere one end to back of image panel. In the same manner, insert and secure remaining length of ribbon through lower slit. Using foam squares, attach image panel to olive green rectangle as shown; wrap and secure ends of ribbons to back of rectangle.

Stamp "Swing by sometime!" onto olive green card stock. Punch stamped area with 1-inch circle punch. Adhere to image panel as shown.

Pierce three holes through olive green rectangle next to upper left corner of image panel and one hole through lower right corner of olive green rectangle. Attach brads. Using foam squares, attach olive green rectangle centered to card front. ✗

Sources: Card stock, punches and brads from Stampin' Up!; printed papers from 7gypsies; stamp set from Flourishes; Copic markers from Imagination International Inc.

Materials

- Card stock: dark red, olive green, cream
- Gypsy Market double-sided printed papers: Sharne, Herne, Saigie
- Swing Set stamp set
- Black dye ink pad
- Alcohol-based-ink markers: grayish yellow, pale olive, marine green, lipstick red, dark red, caramel, pale sepia, brick beige, sand, light walnut, brown
- 8 inches ⅜-inch-wide olive green chenille-dot ribbon
- 6 fall-colored small round brads
- Punches: 1-inch circle, Slit
- Piercing tool
- Sewing machine with cream thread
- Adhesive foam squares
- Paper adhesive

Dogwood Sympathy

Design by **Debbie Olson**

Cut a 5¼ x 4-inch card base from kraft card stock; round corners. Set aside.

Using dark brown ink, stamp dogwood image twice onto cream card stock. Using alcohol-based-ink markers, color only the blossom on one image; cut out. In the same manner, color all except the blossom on second image. Outline outer edges of blossom with markers. Cut out second image around outer oval border; ink edges light brown. Using foam tape, adhere blossom over intact dogwood image. Detail leaves and blossom center with glitter pens.

Using Labels Ten die template, die-cut a 3½ x 2¼-inch label from dark brown card stock. Paint outer edge with gold paint marker. Attach dogwood oval to label using foam tape. Place light brown pearls at top and bottom of label. Attach to left side of card base using foam tape only on top half of label. Do not apply foam tape to bottom half of label as this area needs to be kept free so card base will slide into card pocket properly.

Cut a 5½ x 6-inch piece of dark brown card stock; round top two corners. Using dark brown ink, stamp lower 1¾ inches with Turning A New Leaf. Score a line 1¾ inches above bottom edge; fold as shown, forming a pocket.

Cut two 1 x 1¾-inch pieces of dark brown card stock. Fold each piece in half to form two ½ x 1¾-inch side pieces for inside of card pocket. Adhere folded pieces to inside of card pocket with folded edges flush with sides and bottom edges flush with fold of pocket.

Wrap ribbon around card pocket as shown; adhere as needed. Using dark brown ink, stamp sentiments onto right side of card base as shown. Slide card base into card pocket allowing bottom half of dogwood label to slide over ribbon as shown. ✘

Sources: Card stock and Turning A New Leaf, With Sympathy and Communiqué Sentiments stamp sets from Papertrey Ink.; Beautiful Blossoms stamp set from JustRite; Copic markers and Spica glitter pens from Imagination International Inc.; gold paint marker from Elmer's® Products Inc.; die template from Spellbinders™ Paper Arts.

Materials

- Card stock: cream, dark brown, kraft
- Stamp sets: Beautiful Blossoms, Turning A New Leaf, With Sympathy, Communiqué Sentiments
- Ink pads: dark brown, light brown
- Alcohol-based-ink markers: colorless blender, warm gray No. 1, warm gray No. 3, pea green, putty, peach, snow green, chamois, milky white, raw silk
- Glitter pens: clear, light green
- Gold paint marker
- 18 inches ½-inch-wide dark brown satin ribbon
- 2 light brown self-adhesive pearls
- Corner rounder punch
- Labels Ten die template (#S5-022)
- Die-cutting machine
- Scoring tool
- Adhesive foam tape
- Paper adhesive

With sympathy

Materials

- Watercolor paper
- Card stock: cream, red
- Double-sided printed papers: Early Bird Cherry Pie, Lil' Man Dapper Dan
- Dog Gone Cute stamp set
- Ink pads: dark brown, light brown, red
- Alcohol-based-ink markers: colorless blender, cool gray No. 00, cool gray No. 1, cool gray No. 3, warm gray No. 0, warm gray No. 1, warm gray No. 2, snow green, pale aqua, ice ocean, abyss green, pale fruit pink, skin white, pink flamingo, prawn, sand white, clay
- 8 inches ⅝-inch-wide red/white stitched grosgrain ribbon
- Cream string
- Aqua button
- Clear glitter glue
- Textured cloth
- Sewing machine with cream thread
- Adhesive foam tape
- Adhesive foam dots
- Paper adhesive

Friends See Heart to Heart

Design by Debbie Olson

Form a 5¼ x 5¼-inch top-folded card from cream card stock.

Cut a 5 x 5-inch square from Cherry Pie paper; adhere to red card stock; trim a small border.

Adhere a 5 x 1¾-inch strip Dapper Dan paper to a 5 x 1⅞-inch strip of red card stock. Adhere layered strip to Cherry Pie square ½ inch from bottom edge. Zigzag-stitch top and bottom edges of layered strip. Place ribbon on layered square as shown; wrap and secure left end to back. Fold right end of ribbon under itself forming a loop; secure with adhesive dot. Adhere piece centered to card front.

Using dark brown ink, stamp boy and dog onto a 3 x 3⅜-inch piece of watercolor paper; color using markers. When dry, dampen textured cloth with colorless blender and dab overalls to fade ink. Ink edges light brown. Add glitter glue to dog's nose. Adhere colored image to red card stock; trim a small border. Machine-stitch around outside edge of image panel. Using foam tape, attach to card front as shown.

Stamp "Friends" onto watercolor paper with red ink; trim around sentiment. Ink edges light brown. Referring to photo, adhere to card front. Thread button with string; tie knot on back and trim ends. Adhere button to ribbon loop as shown. ✗

Sources: Card stock from Papertrey Ink; printed papers from Cosmo Cricket; stamp from My Favorite Things; Copic markers from Imagination International Inc.

Sharing a Cookie

Design by **Broni Holcombe**

Form a 5½ x 4¼-inch top-folded card from white card stock.

Cut a 5⅝ x 4⅛-inch rectangle from Vintage Plaid paper. Adhere centered to card front. Wrap ribbon around card front as shown; tie bow on left side and trim ends.

Using Labels One die template, die-cut a 3⅞-inch label from white card stock and a 3⅜-inch label from Admiral paper. Adhere Admiral label to white label; attach to right side of card front.

Using computer and printer, print Bronte and Louis digital image onto detail blending paper. Color image with markers; detail hair and chocolate on mouth with colored pencil. Cut out image. Attach to card front as shown with foam tape. Die-cut a tag from white card stock using Tiny Tags die template. Stamp "Happy Day!" onto tag. String tag and button with twine; tie knot; trim ends. Adhere button to center of bow on card front. ✗

Sources: *Detail blending paper and card stock from Couture Cardstock; printed papers from BasicGrey; digital stamp from Mo's Digital Pencil; stamp from Our Craft Lounge; Copic markers from Imagination International Inc.; colored pencil from Prismacolor; Labels One die template from Spellbinders™ Paper Arts; Tiny Tags die template from Provo Craft.*

Materials

- Detail blending paper
- White card stock
- June Bug double-sided printed papers: Vintage Plaid, Admiral
- Bronte and Louis digital stamp
- Golfin Gramps stamp
- Black fine-detail pigment ink pad
- Alcohol-based-ink markers: black, warm gray No. 00, warm gray No. 0, warm gray No. 1, warm gray No. 5, neutral gray No. 1, neutral gray No. 4, neutral gray No. 7, frost blue, light crockery blue, yellow-green, yellow fluorite, pinkish white, blush, prawn, light prawn, lipstick red, baby skin pink, pale fruit pink, pink flamingo, brick beige, milky white, lily white, sand white, skin white
- Chocolate colored pencil
- 23 inches ⅝-inch-wide olive satin ribbon
- Twine
- Red large round button
- Die templates: Labels One (#S4-161), Tiny Tags (#37-1222)
- Die-cutting machine
- Adhesive foam tape
- Paper adhesive
- Computer with printer

Thanks

Design by **Sherrie Siemens**

Form a 4¼ x 5½-inch side-folded card from light green card stock.

Cut a 3½ x 5½-inch piece of Wood Veneer paper. Using brown ink, stamp "thanks" onto lower right corner. Adhere to card front as shown.

Wrap ribbon around card front as shown; tie a bow at top; trim ends.

Using watermark ink, stamp Fawn in the Grove onto smooth white card stock. Sprinkle clear embossing powder over image and emboss using embossing heat tool. Color image with markers.

Using Labels Twelve die template, die-cut a 3⅛-inch label around stamped area. Leaving die template in place, color background of label using dull ivory marker and airbrush system. Using foam tape, attach label to card front as shown. ✗

Sources: *Real Wood paper from Creative Imaginations; stamps from Cornish Heritage Farms; watermark ink pad from Tsukineko LLC; Copic markers and Copic Airbrush System from Imagination International Inc.*

Materials

- Card stock: light green, smooth white
- Real Wood Veneer paper
- Stamps: Fawn in the Grove, Silhouette Blooms II set
- Ink pads: brown, watermark
- Clear embossing powder
- Alcohol-based-ink markers: brick beige, chamois, sepia, dull ivory, clay, pale porcelain blue, pea green, moss, yellow green, blush
- 18½ inches ¼-inch-wide light green satin ribbon
- Labels Twelve die template (#S4-247)
- Die-cutting machine
- Airbrush system
- Embossing heat tool
- Adhesive foam squares
- Paper adhesive

Materials

- Card stock: cream, lavender, pink, smooth white
- Special Delivery stamp set
- Dye ink pads: black, brown
- Alcohol-based-ink markers: rose pink, rose mist, rose red, colorless blender, pale thistle, viola, floral white, bisque, brick beige
- Opaque white pigment paint
- 16 inches ⅜-inch-wide white grosgrain ribbon
- White string
- Purple button
- Labels One die template (#S4-161)
- Die-cutting machine
- Paintbrush
- Craft sponge
- Double-sided tape
- Adhesive foam squares
- Paper adhesive

Special Delivery

Design by **Jeanne Streiff**

Form a 5½ x 4¼-inch top-folded card from cream card stock; ink edges brown.

Using black ink, stamp "Special Delivery" onto lower right corner of a 5½ x 2⅛-inch piece of lavender card stock. Ink edges brown and adhere to card front as shown.

Wrap an 11-inch length of ribbon around card front, over top edge of lavender card-stock piece; wrap and secure ends to back. Form a ribbon loop with remaining length of ribbon; adhere to left side of card front as shown. String button with white string; tie knot on top and trim ends. Adhere button over ribbon loop as shown.

Using Labels One die template, die-cut a 2⅞-inch label from pink card stock and a 2⅜-inch label from white card stock. Ink edges of pink label brown; attach to card front as shown using foam squares.

Using black ink, stamp a postage stamp frame, baby carriage and other postage images onto white label. Color baby carriage stamp and label background as desired with markers. Paint white dots onto baby carriage stamp; let dry completely. Adhere to pink label as shown. ✘

Sources: *Card stock from Couture Cardstock; stamp set from Gina K. Designs; Copic markers and pigment paint from Imagination International Inc.; die template from Spellbinders™ Paper Arts.*

Birthday Bloomers

Design by **Trudy Sjolander**

Form a 4¼ x 5½-inch top-folded card from smooth white card stock.

Using embossing machine and Swiss Dots embossing folder, emboss a 3½ x 4⅞-inch piece of smooth white card stock. Adhere to a 4 x 5¼-inch piece of lavender pearlescent card stock. Use sewing machine to zigzag-stitch along edge of embossed piece. Wrap a 6-inch length of ribbon around layered card-stock piece as shown; secure ends to back. Pierce a hole through each corner of embossed piece; insert brads. Adhere panel centered to card front.

Using black ink, stamp flowerpot twice onto smooth white card stock. In the same manner, stamp flowers over both flowerpots. Stamp flowers onto a piece of smooth white card stock two more times.

Using Standard Circles LG die template, die-cut a 2⅜-inch circle around one flowerpot with flowers stamped on top of it.

Color all flowers and flowerpots with markers, using colorless blender when needed. Add a shadow underneath die-cut flowerpot. Ink edges of die-cut piece with lavender and purple inks, using purple ink along outer edge.

Cut out second flowerpot with flowers and first bunch of flowers. Cut second bunch of flowers into separate flower layers as desired. Using foam tape, adhere layers to die-cut image. Add glitter glue to flowers using small paintbrush. In the same manner, apply clear glaze medium to leaves.

Using Classic Scalloped Circles SM die template, die-cut a 2⅞-inch scalloped circle from green pearlescent card stock. Adhere stamped die-cut circle to scalloped circle. Using foam tape, attach to card front as shown.

Using black ink, stamp "Happy Birthday" onto smooth white card stock. Die-cut sentiment using 1 x 1-inch Classic Squares LG die template. Ink edges in the same manner as for die-cut circle.

Die-cut a 1⅛ x 1⅛-inch scalloped square from green pearlescent card stock using Classic Scalloped Squares LG die template. Adhere sentiment square to scalloped square. Adhere to center top of card front on top of ribbon.

Tie a bow with remaining ribbon; trim ends. Adhere to card front centered below flowerpot. ✗

Sources: Smooth white card stock from Neenah Paper Inc.; pearlescent card stock from Paper Temptress; Bless My Bloomers stamp set from Clear Dollar Stamps; chalk ink pads from Clearsnap Inc.; die templates from Spellbinders™ Paper Arts; Cuttlebug machine and embossing folder from Provo Craft; Stickles glitter glue from Ranger Industries Inc.; clear dimensional glaze medium from JudiKins Inc.

Materials

- Card stock: smooth white, lavender pearlescent, green pearlescent
- Bless My Bloomers stamp set
- Black dye ink pad
- Chalk ink pads: purple, lavender
- Alcohol-based-ink markers: colorless blender, lime green, pale yellow, chamois, chrome orange, brown, peach, amethyst, mauve shadow, yellow
- 14 inches ⅜-inch-wide purple sheer ribbon
- 4 purple small round brads
- Die templates: Standard Circles LG (#S4-116), Classic Scalloped Circles SM (#S4-125), Classic Squares LG (#S4-126), Classic Scalloped Squares LG (#S4-127)
- Swiss Dots embossing folder (#37-1604)
- Die-cutting and embossing machine
- Small paintbrush
- Piercing tool
- Sewing machine with green thread
- Clear glitter glue
- Clear dimensional glaze medium
- Adhesive foam tape
- Paper adhesive

Materials

- Card stock: cream, red, turquoise
- The Thrift Shop double-sided printed papers: Near Mint, One-of-a-Kind
- Masking paper
- Enjoy The Ride stamp set
- Dye ink pads: black, red, light brown
- Turquoise chalk pigment ink pad
- Alcohol-based-ink markers: colorless blender, warm gray No. 2, warm gray No. 3, cool gray No. 0, cool gray No. 1, cool gray No. 2, cool gray No. 4, cool gray No. 6, mint green, Nile blue, duck blue, golden yellow, yellowish beige
- 7 inches ⅝-inch-wide turquoise grosgrain ribbon
- 2 silver small round brads
- Die templates: Classic Squares SM (#S4-128), Double Ended Tags (#S3-149)
- Die-cutting machine
- Airbrush system
- Piercing tool
- Sewing machine with cream thread
- Adhesive foam tape
- Paper adhesive

Enjoy the Ride

Design by **Debbie Olson**

Form a 5 x 5-inch top-folded card from cream card stock.

Adhere a 4¾ x 4¾-inch piece of Near Mint paper to turquoise card stock; trim a small border. Wrap ribbon around layered piece ¾ inch from bottom edge; secure ends to back.

Adhere a 4¾ x 2-inch strip of One-of-a-Kind paper to a 4¾ x 2⅛-inch piece of red card stock. Using sewing machine, zigzag-stitch top and bottom edges. Adhere to layered piece as shown.

Using black ink, stamp car image onto cream card stock and onto masking paper. Using markers, color cream card-stock image. Cut out masking image.

Using Classic Squares SM die template, die-cut a 2¾ x 2¾-inch square around colored image. Leaving die template in place, carefully position masking image over colored image. Using markers and airbrush system, color background of die-cut piece, adding a shadow as desired. Remove die template and mask; ink edges light brown. Adhere die-cut piece to red card stock; trim a small border. Using foam tape, attach to layered piece as shown.

Using red ink, stamp "enjoy" onto cream card stock. Using turquoise ink, stamp "THE RIDE" next to "enjoy."

Using Double Ended Tags die template, die-cut a 2¾ x ⅝ tag around sentiment. Ink edges light brown. Using foam tape, attach to bottom of die-cut square as shown. Pierce a hole through both sides of sentiment tag, going through all layers of layered piece; attach brads. Adhere centered to card front. ✘

Sources: Card stock and Enjoy The Ride stamp set from Papertrey Ink; printed papers from October Afternoon; chalk pigment ink pad from Tsukineko LLC; Copic markers and Copic Airbrush System from Imagination International Inc.; die templates from Spellbinders™ Paper Arts.

Materials

- Card stock: gray, light peach, teal, white
- Ooh La La For Him double-sided printed papers: Frivolous, Soiree
- Sing to the Lord stamp set
- Black dye ink pad
- Alcohol-based-ink markers: warm gray No. 1, warm gray No. 2, warm gray No. 3, warm gray No. 7, snow green, sea green, emerald green, moon white, bronze, golden yellow, honey, maize, loquat, cadmium orange
- 12½ inches ⅜-inch-wide white taffeta ribbon
- Teal self-adhesive pearls: 2 small, 2 medium, 2 large
- Labels Four die template (#S4-190)
- Die-cutting machine
- Adhesive foam squares
- Paper adhesive

I Will Sing

Design by **Christine Okken**

Form a 4¼ x 5½-inch top-folded card from gray card stock.

Cut a 4 x 5⅛-inch rectangle from Frivolous paper. Adhere to teal card stock; trim a small border.

Dye entire length of white ribbon by coloring ribbon with moon white marker. Cut a 5½-inch length of ribbon; wrap around center of layered rectangle; secure ends to back. Tie bow with remaining ribbon; trim ends; set aside.

Using Labels Four die template, die-cut two 2¾ x 4⅜-inch labels from Soiree paper. Cut labels in half; adhere a piece from each label together as shown. Adhere to light peach card stock; trim a

small border. Using foam squares, attach to layered rectangle.

Stamp bird on branch and flower branch onto white card stock. Die-cut area around bird on branch using a 2¼ x 3⅝-inch Labels Four die template. Using markers, color stamped images adding a soft outline around die-cut image. Cut out flower branch. Use foam squares to attach flower branch to die-cut image as shown. Adhere assembled image onto layered rectangle as shown. Adhere to card front.

Stamp "I will sing" on lower left corner of card front. Attach bow and pearls to card front as shown. ✘

Sources: *Card stock from Stampin' Up!, Bazzill Basics Paper Inc. and Flourishes; printed papers from My Mind's Eye; stamp set from Our Daily Bread designs; Copic markers from Imagination International Inc.; die template from Spellbinders™ Paper Arts.*

Make a Wish

Design by **Debbie Olson**

Form a 5½ x 4¼-inch top-folded card from kraft card stock; round bottom two corners of card front and back.

Cut a 5⅜ x 4⅛-inch rectangle from aqua printed paper; round bottom two corners; sand edges. Cut a 5⅜ x 2½-inch strip of striped printed paper; sand edges. Adhere strip to aqua rectangle as shown. Using sewing machine, zigzag-stitch top and bottom edges of striped strip. Wrap twill around rectangle as shown; secure ends to back.

Cut six 16-inch lengths of twine. Holding twine lengths together, wrap around twill on rectangle; tie in knot. Adhere layered rectangle centered to card front.

Using black ink, stamp beach chair image and desired border onto white card stock; color both images with markers.

Using Classic Ovals die template, die-cut a 2¾ x 2-inch oval from stamped beach chair image. Leaving oval die template in place, airbrush sky using pale blue marker and airbrush system. Detail image using glitter, glitter pens and gold metallic marker.

Using Labels Ten die template, die-cut a 3½ x 2¼-inch label around border image. Ink edges of both die-cut images light brown. Using foam tape, attach oval die cut centered to label die cut. Attach layered die cuts to card front as shown using foam tape.

Using blue ink, stamp "make a Wish" onto white card stock. Die-cut sentiment with smallest Double Ended

Tags die template; ink edges light brown. Insert safety pin through tag hole and attach to twine knot on card front.

String buttons with twine; tie knots on back and trim ends. Adhere buttons to card front as shown. ✗

Sources: Card stock, Mixed Messages stamp set and buttons from Papertrey Ink; Sea Glass Mat Pad from K&Company; By The Sea stamp set from JustRite; Copic markers, Spica glitter pens and Copic Airbrush System from Imagination International Inc.; gold metallic marker from EK Success; die templates from Spellbinders™ Paper Arts.

Materials

- Card stock: kraft, white
- Sea Glass Mat Pad
- Stamp sets: By The Sea, Mixed Messages
- Ink pads: black dye, light brown dye, blue pigment
- Alcohol-based-ink markers: colorless blender, snow green, moon white, horizon green, pale blue, anise, pea green, Napoli yellow, buttercup yellow, light suntan, reddish brass, brick white, sand white, neutral gray No. 1, cool gray No. 0, cool gray No. 2
- Gold metallic marker
- Glitter pens: clear, green
- White iridescent glitter
- Twine
- 7 inches ¾-inch-wide natural twill
- 2 light aqua buttons
- Small antique brass safety pin
- Corner rounder punch
- Die templates: Double Ended Tags (#S3-149), Classic Ovals SM (#S4-112), Labels Ten (#S5-022)
- Die-cutting machine
- Airbrush system
- Sewing machine with cream thread
- Sandpaper
- Adhesive foam tape
- Paper adhesive

Garden Thanks

Design by **Jeanne Streiff**

Form a 4¼ x 5½-inch top-folded card from brown card stock. Using aqua blue marker, color a 4⅛ x 5⅜-inch panel of smooth white card stock. Apply colorless blender marker to soft cloth; dab colored panel with cloth; repeat as desired. Ink edges brown and adhere centered to card front.

Using black ink, stamp garden planter onto a 3¼ x 4⅜-inch piece of smooth white card stock. Color with markers, blending colors with colorless blender. Using black ink, stamp "thanks" under garden planter as shown. Ink edges brown and adhere to brown card stock; trim a small border. Adhere gold beads to upper left corner of white card stock as shown. Using foam squares, attach layered piece centered to card front. ✗

Sources: *Card stock from Couture Cardstock; stamps from Impression Obsession Inc.; Copic markers from Imagination International Inc.*

Materials

- Card stock: brown, smooth white
- Stamps: Garden Planter, Sentiments I set
- Dye ink pads: black, brown
- Alcohol-based-ink markers: aqua blue, pumpkin yellow, sanguine, yellowish beige, chartreuse, pea green, lime green, ocean green, sardonyx, pale aqua, snow green, brick beige, sand, reddish brown, burnt sienna, light mahogany, colorless blender, warm gray No. 1, warm gray No. 3, warm gray No. 5
- 3 gold self-adhesive flat-back beads
- Soft cloth
- Craft sponge
- Adhesive foam squares
- Paper adhesive

Materials

- Card stock: cream, dark red, black
- Stamps: Ornament set, Cover-a-Card Music, Cover-a-Card Flourishes
- Chalk ink pads: dark gray, dark red, light brown
- Alcohol-based-ink markers: colorless blender, dark red
- 22 inches ½-inch-wide dark red/white-dot ribbon
- Gold photo hanger
- 3 black small round brads
- Die templates: Classic Scalloped Rectangles LG (#S4-143), Deckle Mega Rectangles SM (#S5-014), Labels Nine (#S4-233)
- Die-cutting machine
- Piercing tool
- Craft sponge
- Small adhesive dots
- Adhesive foam squares
- Paper adhesive

Ornamental Joy

Design by **Keri Lee Sereika**

Form a 7 x 5-inch top-folded card from dark red card stock.

Using light brown ink, stamp Cover-a-Card Music onto a 6¾ x 4¾-inch piece of cream card stock as shown; ink edges light brown. Adhere a 6¾ x ¾-inch strip of black card stock to cream piece 1 inch above bottom edge.

Die-cut a ⅞ x ⅞-inch Labels Nine tag from cream card stock. Using black ink, stamp "joy" onto tag; ink edges light brown. Pierce a hole through top of tag; slide a black brad through photo hanger and tag hole; secure brad closed.

Wrap ribbon around black card-stock strip as shown. Slide photo hanger onto ribbon; tie into a bow and trim ends. Secure bow to black strip using an adhesive dot. Adhere cream card-stock piece centered to card front. Pierce a hole in upper two corners; attach brads.

Die-cut a 2⅝ x 5¼-inch scalloped rectangle from dark red card stock. Using foam squares, attach to card front as shown.

Die-cut a 2⅛ x 4½-inch deckle rectangle from cream card stock. Using black ink, stamp three ornaments onto rectangle; color with dark red marker. Stamp bows onto tops of ornaments using dark red ink.

In the same manner, stamp three more ornaments onto a piece of cream card sock; color with dark red marker. Color Cover-a-Card Flourish stamp with colorless blender and immediately stamp onto colored ornaments. Cut out round part of colored ornaments. Using foam squares, attach over ornaments on deckle rectangle. Use foam squares to attach deckle rectangle to card front as shown. ✘

Sources: Card stock from Bazzill Basics Paper Inc.; stamps from Impression Obsession Inc.; chalk ink pads from Clearsnap Inc.; Copic markers from Imagination International Inc.; die templates from Spellbinders™ Paper Arts.

Birthday Wishes

Design by **Debbie Olson**

Form a 4 x 4-inch top-folded card from white card stock.

Cut a 3⅞ x 3⅞-inch square from pink printed paper and a 3⅞ x 1⅜-inch strip from light yellow printed paper. Using largest Labels Eight die template, die-cut bottom edges of both cut pieces and card base.

Adhere a 3⅞ x ¾-inch strip of green printed paper to pink piece 2 inches above die-cut edge. Adhere light yellow die-cut strip to pink square below green strip as shown.

Machine-stitch along top edge of green strip and along bottom edge of light yellow strip; zigzag-stitch between strips. Adhere pink piece to card front.

Using Labels One die template, die-cut a 2⅜-inch label from white card stock; ink edges light brown. Using foam tape, attach centered to card front.

Stamp "birthday WISHES" onto white card stock with pink ink. Trim around sentiment to create a tag, leaving room on left end for a hole; ink edges light brown. Punch a ⅛-inch hole through left end of tag. Thread string through tag hole; set aside.

Punch a ⅛-inch hole on right side of card front, 1½ inches from bottom edge and ½ inch from right edge. Wrap ribbon around card front as shown, placing loose ends on right side. The ribbon will cover the hole.

Slide one end of string attached to sentiment tag through hole on card front, around ribbon inside card and back though hole. Tie string ends together into a bow around ribbon; trim ends. Secure tag with a foam dot.

Using dark brown ink, stamp cupcake onto white card stock and green, light yellow and pink printed papers. Cut off leaves from green cupcake, top part of cupcake from pink cupcake and cupcake base from light yellow cupcake. Cut out entire white card-stock cupcake. Referring to photo, adhere cupcake pieces to white card-stock cupcake.

Using gray markers, color a shadow on left side of layered cupcake; add yellow and pink shading as needed. Blend colors with colorless blender. Apply glue from glue pen along scalloped edge of cupcake; add glitter. Thread button with string; tie knot on back and trim ends. Adhere button to cupcake as shown.

Using foam dots, attach cupcake to card front as shown. Use gray markers to color a shadow below cupcake. ✘

Sources: *Card stock, Pretty Pastels Pad and stamp sets from Papertrey Ink; Copic markers from Imagination International Inc.; die templates from Spellbinders™ Paper Arts.*

Materials

- White card stock
- Pretty Pastels Pad
- Stamp sets: Baby Button Bits, Mega Mixed Messages
- Ink pads: pink, dark brown, light brown
- Alcohol-based-ink markers: colorless blender, warm gray No. 00, warm gray No. 1, pale yellowish pink, light reddish yellow
- 9 inches ⅜-inch-wide pink twill ribbon
- Cream string
- Pink button
- Clear glitter
- ⅛-inch hole punch
- Die templates: Labels One (#S4-161), Labels Eight (#S5-019)
- Die-cutting machine
- Sewing machine with cream thread
- Adhesive foam tape
- Adhesive foam dots
- Glue pen
- Paper adhesive

Sweet Peas

Design by **Christine Okken**

Form a 5½ x 4¼-inch side-folded card from light brown card stock. Cut a 5⅜ x 4⅛-inch rectangle from Eloquent paper; adhere to card front as shown.

Cut a 4¼ x 3-inch rectangle from Winsome paper. Adhere to light brown card stock; trim a small border. Adhere centered to card front.

Cut a 5⅜ x 1⅞-inch strip of Vivacious paper. Cut a 5⅜ x 1-inch strip of light brown card stock; punch bottom edge with Pinking Hearts border punch. Adhere light brown strip to bottom edge of Vivacious strip on reverse side as shown. Insert ribbon through ribbon slide; wrap ribbon around strip; secure ends to back. Adhere to card front ⅝ inch from bottom edge.

Using black ink, stamp sweet peas onto a 2⅞ x 2⅜-inch piece of white card stock. Color sweet peas with markers, adding a soft outline around image. Using pink ink, stamp "Sweet Peas" onto upper left edge of image panel. Adhere panel to light brown card stock; trim a small border. Pierce a hole through lower right corner of image panel; attach brad. Using foam squares, attach image panel to card front as shown. ✗

Sources: *Card stock from Bazzill Basics Paper Inc.; printed papers from SEI; stamp set, decorative brad and ribbon slide from Flourishes; border punch from Stampin' Up!; Copic markers from Imagination International Inc.*

Materials

- Card stock: light brown, smooth white
- Claire double-sided printed papers: Winsome, Vivacious, Eloquent
- Sweet Peas stamp set
- Dye ink pads: black, pink
- Alcohol-based-ink markers: pink beryl, pinkish vanilla, light tea rose, light rouge, pinkish white, pale cherry pink, dim green, spring dim green, verdigris
- 8 inches 1¼-inch-wide pink silk ribbon
- Silver decorative brad
- Silver ribbon slide
- Pinking Hearts border punch
- Piercing tool
- Adhesive foam squares
- Paper adhesive

Fall Floral

Design by **Debbie Olson**

Form a 4¼ x 5½-inch top-folded card from cream card stock.

Cut a 4 x 5¼-inch piece from polka-dot paper. Adhere a 4 x 1½-inch strip of floral paper and a 4 x 3-inch strip of leaves paper to polka-dot piece as shown. Machine-stitch along top edges of both strips; zigzag-stitch along bottom edges of both strips. Adhere a 4 x 2⅛-inch strip of striped paper, centered to leaves strip.

Wrap lace around bottom edge of striped strip; secure ends to back. Adhere layered piece to orange card stock; trim a small border. Adhere centered to card front.

Wrap orange ribbon around card front above lace; tie in a bow on right side; trim ends.

Using black ink, stamp a flower and three leaves onto cream card stock; color with markers. Detail center of flower with clear embossing liquid; let dry completely. Cut out leaves and flower; ink edges light brown. Using foam tape, attach leaves and flower to card front as shown. ✘

Sources: *Card stock, printed papers and stamp set from Papertrey Ink; Copic markers from Imagination International Inc.; Glossy Accents clear embossing liquid from Ranger Industries Inc.*

Materials

- Card stock: white, cream, orange
- Autumn Abundance printed papers: floral, polka-dot, leaves, striped
- Friends 'Til The End stamp set
- Ink pads: black, light brown
- Alcohol-based-ink markers: colorless blender, warm gray No. 00, warm gray No. 1, loquat, pumpkin yellow, sanguine, grayish yellow, pale olive, Spanish olive
- Clear embossing liquid
- Ribbons: 15 inches ½-inch-wide orange satin, 6 inches ½-inch-wide cream lace
- Sewing machine with cream thread
- Adhesive foam tape
- Paper adhesive

Beyond the Basics

Color is my daylong obsession, joy and torment.

—**Claude Monet**

Bringing your stamped and colored images to their full potential is easily achieved. By simply adding highlights to your image with a white gel pen, lightly dusting a small fairy with sparkly glitter, or by using dimensional paint for just a touch of texture, an already beautiful image can be elevated to a whole new level. In this bonus section we are going to showcase all of these techniques, and more, using project examples from each of the previous chapters.

On her Baby's Window card, Kathy Menzies gave the tail on the cute bunny a little texture using a bit of Flower Soft and highlighted the cloud using a bit of glitter glue.

On the Swing By Sometime card, Christine Okken used a very specific technique known as pointillism. For this application, the image is colored with only the tip of the marker to dot on color. Leaving a small amount of white space between in dots allows room to change colors and create depth.

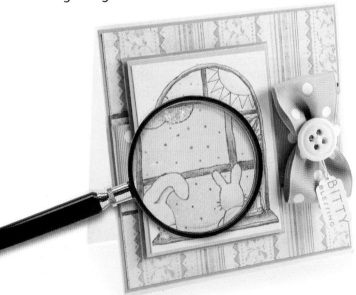

Adding texture and design can be accomplished in in various ways. For the Ornamental Joy card, Keri Lee Sereika colored in each ornament completely using a dark-colored alcohol-based-ink marker. A colorless blender marker was then used to moisten the surface of a rubber stamp, and the image was stamped onto each colored ornament. The colorless blender solution will remove the color, leaving the stamped design behind.

For the Birthday Wishes card, Debbie Olson first stamped the main image onto patterned paper, and then used alcohol markers to shade and enhance. Images with larger, more open areas work well for this technique—think shirts, dresses, cupcakes and similar-type designs that would otherwise be void of detail.

Using a similar technique as the project above, Debbie Olson created interesting texture on the Friends See Heart to Heart card using a small scrap of textured fabric saturated with colorless blending solution. By touching the cloth to the solidly colored portions of the little boy's overalls as well as to the fur of the dog she achieved a perfect faint texture.

Once again using patterned paper for inspiration, Christine Okken colored not only the main image of the I Will Sing card using alcohol markers but also colored her white ribbon aqua to make a custom-dyed embellishment. Many items such as pearls, gems and brad heads can be colored using alcohol markers to craft perfectly matching accents.

Another wonderful way to add a finishing touch to a colored image is to apply a paper gloss to parts of the image. Here Trudy Sjolander embellished the image on the A Little Something card by cutting out and layering different parts of the image. She also applied paper gloss and a bit of glitter to the surface of the balloon to really accentuate it.

On this For You note card, Dawn Lusk stamped and colored her image and then stamped over top of it again using a stamp positioner to recapture the detail of the image after it was colored. She then created an embossed oval frame to perfectly emphasize the image as a whole.

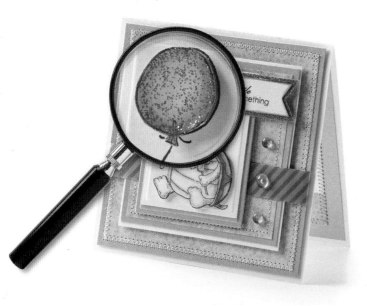

Kathy Menzies' Secret Fishing Spot card is a great example of how to create a custom background by stamping with white pigment ink and then brayering over that with a deep-colored dye ink, creating a resist type of background.

Dawn Lusk used a few techniques to make the image on her Chickadee card really stand out. She colored her main image and outlined around the bird using coordinating colors to create a color-wash background. She then emphasized the white of the bird's chest with a white gel pen and blended that ink to re-highlight that part of her image.

Designers

Asela Hopkins
www.hopartstudios.typepad.com

Special Friend, 11   Blue Hydrangea, 13

Broni Holcombe
www.bronih.typepad.com/splashesofwatercolor

Duet Hi, 29   Floral Trio, 36
Shopping Granny, 30   Sharing a Cookie, 61

Chrissy Le
www.paperinkcolor.blogspot.com

Pixie Thinking of You, 14   Beary Happy Birthday, 21

Christine Okken
http://christinecreations.blogspot.com

Stargazer Lilies, 46   I Will Sing, 67
Swing By Sometime, 57   Sweet Peas, 74

Dawn Lusk
www.dawnanewday.blogspot.com

Fond Memories, 16   Tender Thoughts, 35
Chickadee, 34   For You, 40

Debbie Olson
www.debbiedesigns.typepad.com

Daisies & Roses, 19   Enjoy the Ride, 66
Thank You Butterflies, 32   Make a Wish, 68
Geranium Get Well, 56   Birthday Wishes, 72
Dogwood Sympathy, 58   Fall Floral, 75
Friends See Heart to Heart, 60

Jeanne Streiff
www.inkypaws.blogs.splitcoaststampers.com

Fairy Thanks, 10   Special Delivery, 63
Thank You, 37   Garden Thanks, 70

Kathy Menzies
www.thecreataholic.blogspot.com

Baby's Window, 8   True Friend, 22
Jeweled Peony, 12   Secret Fishing Spot, 44

Keri Lee Sereika
www.pinklemonade.typepad.com

Happy Birthday Fishes, 6   Hap-bee Day, 28
You're Too Cool!, 7   Pineapple Welcome, 54
Simple Argyle, 18   Ornamental Joy, 71
Meowy Christmas, 20

Laurie Wilson
www.clearlydelightful.typepad.com/clearly_delightful

Vintage Christmas, 48

Sherrie Siemens
www.sherrie-cardcreme.blogspot.com

Thanks, 62

Trudy Sjolander
www.truesgiftsfromtheheart.blogspot.com

Warm Fuzzies, 31   A Little Something, 42
We Heard the Buzzzz, 38   Birthday Bloomers, 64
Heartfelt Sympathy, 41

Coloring Techniques for Card Making

EDITOR Tanya Fox

ART DIRECTOR Brad Snow

PUBLISHING SERVICES DIRECTOR Brenda Gallmeyer

ASSOCIATE EDITOR Brooke Smith

ASSISTANT ART DIRECTOR Nick Pierce

COPY SUPERVISOR Michelle Beck

COPY EDITORS Emily Carter, Mary O'Donnell

TECHNICAL EDITOR Corene Painter

PHOTOGRAPHY SUPERVISOR Tammy Christian

PHOTO STYLISTS Tammy Liechty, Tammy Steiner

PHOTOGRAPHY Matthew Owen

PRODUCTION ARTIST SUPERVISOR Erin Augsburger

GRAPHIC ARTIST Nicole Gage

PRODUCTION ASSISTANSTS Marj Morgan, Judy
  Neuenschwander

Library of Congress Control Number: 2010909687
ISBN: 978-1-59635-308-4
Printed in USA
3 4 5 6 7 8 9

Coloring Techniques for Card Making is published by DRG, 306 East Parr Road, Berne, IN 46711. Printed in USA. Copyright © 2010 DRG. All rights reserved. This publication may not be reproduced in part or in whole without written permission from the publisher.

RETAIL STORES: If you would like to carry this pattern book or any other DRG publications, visit DRGwholesale.com

Every effort has been made to ensure that the instructions in this publication are complete and accurate. We cannot, however, take responsibility for human error, typographical mistakes or variations in individual work. Please visit AnniesCustomerCare.com to check for pattern updates.

Buyer's Guide

7gypsies
(877) 412-7467
www.sevengypsies.com

American Crafts Inc.
(801) 226-0747
www.americancrafts.com

BasicGrey
(801) 544-1116
www.basicgrey.com

Bazzill Basics Paper Inc.
(800) 560-1610
www.bazzillbasics.com

Clear Dollar Stamps
(417) 267-7024
www.cleardollarstamps.com

Clearsnap Inc.
(800) 448-4862
www.clearsnap.com

Cornish Heritage Farms
(877) 860-5328
www.cornishheritagefarms.com

Cosmo Cricket
(800) 852-8810
www.cosmocricket.com

Couture Cardstock
www.couturecardstock.com

Creative Imaginations
(800) 942-6487
www.cigift.com

Die Cuts With A View
(801) 224-6766
www.diecutswithaview.com

Ecstasy Crafts Inc.
(888) 288-7131
www.ecstasycrafts.com

EK Success
(800) 794-5866
www.eksuccess.com

Elmer's® Products Inc.
(614) 985-2600
www.elmers.com

Faber-Castell USA Inc.
(800) 642-2288
www.faber-castell.us

Fancy Pants Designs
(801) 779-3212
www.fancypantsdesigns.com

Fiskars
(866) 348-5661
www.fiskarscrafts.com

Flourishes
(850) 475-1500
www.flourishes.org

Flower Soft Inc.
(877) 989-0205
www.flower-soft.com

Georgia-Pacific
www.gp.com

Gina K. Designs
(608) 579-1026
www.ginakdesigns.com

Hero Arts
(800) 822-4376
www.heroarts.com

Hobby Lobby Stores Inc./ The Paper Studio
www.hobbylobby.com

Imagination International Inc.
(541) 684-0013
www.copicmarker.com

Imaginisce
(801) 908-8111
www.imaginisce.com

Impression Obsession Inc.
(877) 259-0905
www.impression-obsession.com

Inkadinkado
(800) 794-5866
www.inkadinkado.com

Innovative Stamp Creations Inc.
www.innovativestampcreations.com

Inky Antics
(800) 945-3980
www.inkyantics.com

Janlynn Corp./Stamps Happen Inc.
www.janlynn.com

JudiKins Inc.
(310) 515-1115
www.judikins.com

JustRite
www.justritestampers.com

KLM Designs
www.klmdigistamps.com

K&Company
(800) 749-5866
www.kandcompany.com

Koh-I-Noor
(800) 628-1910
www.kohinoorusa.com

Lockhart Stamp Co.
(707) 775-4703
www.lockhartstampcompany.com

Lyra
www.lyra.de

Martha Stewart Crafts
(800) 794-5866
www.marthastewartcrafts.com

Memory Box
www.memoryboxco.com

McGill Inc.
(800) 982-9884
www.mcgillinc.com

Mo's Digital Pencil
www.digitalpenciltoo.com

My Favorite Things
www.mftstamps.com

My Mind's Eye
(800) 665-5116
www.mymindseye.com

Neenah Paper Inc.
(800) 994-5993
www.neenahpaper.com

October Afternoon
(866) 513-5553
www.octoberafternoon.com

Our Craft Lounge
(877) 44-LOUNGE
(445-6864)
www.ourcraftlounge.net

Our Daily Bread designs
(216) 401-4124
www.ourdailybreaddesigns.com

Paper Mojo
(800) 420-3818
www.papermojo.com

Paper Temptress
www.papertemptress.com

Papertrey Ink
www.papertreyink.com

Pebbles Inc.
(800) 438-8153
www.pebblesinc.com

Pollycraft
www.pollycraftdesigns.co.uk

Prima Marketing Inc.
(909) 627-5532
www.primamarketinginc.com

Prismacolor
(800) 323-0749
www.prismacolor.com

Provo Craft
(800) 937-7686
www.provocraft.com

Ranger Industries Inc.
(732) 389-3535
www.rangerink.com

The Robin's Nest
(801) 910-8514
www.robinsnest-scrap.com

Rubbernecker Stamp Co.
(909) 263-9322
www.rubbernecker.com

Sakura of America
www.sakuraofamerica.com

Salis International Inc.
(303) 384-3588
www.docmartins.com

Sassy Cheryl's
www.sassycheryls.com

SEI
(800) 333-3279
www.shopsei.com

Sizzix/Ellison
(877) 355-4766
www.sizzix.com

Spellbinders Paper Arts
(888) 547-0400
www.spellbinderspaperarts.com

Stampin' Up!
(800) STAMP UP (782-6787)
www.stampinup.com

Stamp N Plus Scrap N
(715) 271-1873
www.stampaffair.com

Stewart Superior Corp.
(800) 558-2875
www.stewartsuperior.com

Tsukineko LLC
(800) 769-6633
www.tsukineko.com

Waltzingmouse Stamps
www.waltzingmousestamps.com

Webster's Pages
(800) 543-6104
www.websterspages.com

Whipper Snapper Designs Inc.
(262) 938-6824
www.whippersnapperdesigns.com

Yasutomo & Co.
(650) 737-8888
www.yasutomo.com

Zebra Pen Corp
(800) 247-7170
www.zebrapen.com

The Buyer's Guide listings are provided as a service to our readers and should not be considered an endorsement from this publication.